S0-AYZ-951

WEIGHT CONVERSIONS

1 ounce = 28.35 grams

OUNCES	GRAMS
1	28
2	57
3	85
4	113
5	142
6	170
7	198
8 (½ pound)	227
9	255
10	284
11	312
12	340
13	369
14	397
15	425
16 (1 pound)	454
24 (1½ pounds)	680
32 (2 pounds)	907
35.28 (1 kilogram)	1,000
40 (2½ pounds)	1,134
48 (3 pounds)	1,361
64 (4 pounds)	1,814

TEMPERATURE CONVERSIONS

°F to °C = (°F-32) x 0.556

°C to °F = (°C x 1.8) + 32

°F	°C
32 (freezing point of water)	0
70 (room temperature)	21
84 (sour culture "sweet spot")	29
105 (warm water)	41
160 (scald "sweet spot")	71
198 (final bread temperature)	92
212 (boiling point of water)	100
220	105
250	121
300	149
325	163
350	177
375	191
400	205
425	219
450	232
475	246
500	260
525	274
550	288

VOLUME EQUIVALENCIES

3 teaspoons = 1 tablespoon
2 tablespoons = 1 fluid ounce
16 tablespoons = 1 cup
2 cups = 1 pint
2 pints = 1 quart (32 fluid ounces)
4 quarts = 1 gallon

1 teaspoon = 5 milliliters
1 tablespoon = 15 milliliters
1 fluid ounce = 30 milliliters
1 cup = 2.37 deciliters
1 quart = 0.95 liter
1 liter = 33.8 fluid ounces
1 gallon = 3.79 liters

THE RYE BAKER

ALSO BY STANLEY GINSBERG

Inside the Jewish Bakery:
Recipes and Memories from the Golden Age of Jewish Baking
(with Norman Berg)

THE RYE BAKER

Classic Breads from Europe and America

STANLEY GINSBERG

Photographs by Quentin Bacon · Breads by the Author

W. W. Norton & Company

Independent Publishers Since 1923

New York   London

Copyright © 2016 by Stanley Ginsberg

All rights reserved
Printed in China
First Edition

Page 18, ergots on rye head, Connie Strunk, SDSU Extension Plant Pathology Field Specialist,
used with permission; page 21, ergots in malted rye, author; page 42, red rye malt, author.

For information about permission to reproduce selections from this book,
write to Permissions, W. W. Norton & Company, Inc.,
500 Fifth Avenue, New York, NY 10110

For information about special discounts for bulk purchases, please contact
W. W. Norton Special Sales at specialsales@wwnorton.com or 800-233-4830

Manufacturing by RR Donnelley, Shenzhen
Book design by Toni Tajima Design
Production manager: Julia Druskin

ISBN 978-0-393-24521-9

W. W. Norton & Company, Inc.
500 Fifth Avenue, New York, N.Y. 10110
www.wwnorton.com

W. W. Norton & Company Ltd.
Castle House, 75/76 Wells Street, London W1T 3QT

1 2 3 4 5 6 7 8 9 0

For Sylvia, who makes it all worthwhile

Caraway Beer Bread, page 231

Contents

A RYE GEOGRAPHY

In the Nordic countries, dark ryes are perfumed with dill, fennel, anise, and orange. Eastward, in Russia and the Baltics, the breads are caraway-tinged, intensely sour, and austere—*tours de force* of the bakers' mastery of rye's complex chemistry. Along the sandy coastal plains of Holland and Germany, they are dark, sour, and assertive, often with the rustic texture of oilseeds and coarsely milled grain. Farther inland, across the North European Plateau, which extends along the Oder, Elbe, and Vistula Rivers, additions of wheat and spelt turn the breads lighter in color, and the blend of caraway, anise, fennel, and coriander called *brotgewürz* (bread spice) adds its perfume to loaves less assertively sour than their coastal cousins—trends that become more pronounced the farther south one goes.

In France and Spain, rye breads are made using the same baking techniques as for wheat breads; it's the flour that makes them distinctive. In Bavaria and the Alps, the combination of wheat and rye sponges and the liberal use of spices, nuts, and seeds produce a wide range of textures and flavors that are both subtle and complex. And in southern Poland and northern Ukraine, where rye and wheat both grow, white rye flour turns the breads pale and the liberal use of dairy products endows them with mild flavor profiles, against which cumin and tongue-tingling nigella may add a pungent counterpoint.

The Essential Loaf: France and Spain

Rich and Varied: Central and Southwestern Germany

Aromatic and Flavorful: Bavaria, Switzerland, Austria, and Italy

Robust and Complex: Holland, Denmark, and Northern Germany

Tender and Piquant: Southern Poland

Sweet and Crisp: Sweden, Finland, and Iceland

Dark and Intense: Russia and the Baltics

ICELAND

Norwegian Sea

Atlantic Ocean

North Sea

IRELAND

UNITED KINGDOM

THE NETHERLANDS

NORMANDY

Bay of Biscay

FRANCE

PROVENCE

GALICIA

PORTUGAL

SPAIN

Mediterranean Sea

Atlantic Ocean

East Berlin Malt Rye, page 145

The Making of a Rye Baker

*Der Geruch des Brotes ist der Duft aller Düfte. Es ist der Urduft unseres
irdischen Lebens, der Duft der Harmonie, des Friedens und der Heimat.*

The scent of bread is the fragrance of all fragrances; it is the primal fragrance
of our earthly life, the fragrance of harmony, of peace and of home.

—Jaroslav Seifert, 1984 Nobel Laureate in Literature

WHEN I first thought about writing a book on rye bread, I envisioned a foray into the many faces of a largely overlooked grain, at least in North America, that is undergoing a modest renaissance. My journey, however, turned *The Rye Baker* from a baking book into a love story.

I grew up eating rye bread, or at least what I thought of as rye bread—the caraway-seeded deli ryes, the dense gray breads called *corn rye*, which have nothing to do with corn but use the German/Yiddish word *korn*, which means "grain"—and mysteriously dark raisin-flecked pumpernickels my family bought once or twice a week from the Jewish bakeries that dotted the post–World War II Brooklyn neighborhood where I grew up. The breads were a fixture of my childhood, as much as my grandmothers' potato knishes and baked whitefish—things I never thought about until they, along with the bakeries that produced them, faded from my world and from the American foodscape.

To be sure, I could still go into a coffee shop and order a tuna salad on rye or to one of New York's now-disappearing landmark Jewish delis—Katz's, Carnegie, Stage, Lou G. Siegel Gitlitz, and 2nd Ave—for a pastrami, corned beef, or tongue on rye and get an approximation. On closer inspection, however, it was the overwhelming astringency of the caraway that laced the bread, along with heavy slabs of brined meat generously slathered with brown mustard, that lulled me into believing nothing had changed.

But changed it had: those "rye breads" no longer had the robust character that had imprinted itself so indelibly in my taste memory; instead, they'd degenerated into insipid, mass-produced, lowest-common-denominator cushions barely one step removed from supermarket sandwich breads. So far had those traditional breads fallen that William Bernbach, whose advertising agency, Doyle Dane Bernbach, drove Madison Avenue's creative revolution in the 1960s and 1970s, described his client brand, Levy's Real Jewish Rye, as a bread "no Jew would eat."[1]

It was a longing for the tastes of my childhood that drove me to bake my first rye bread. Rye's reputation as a baker's nightmare—sticky, unstable, mercurial in the presence of yeast, as different from wheat as day is from night—daunted me. I still remember the rush of excitement and apprehension that overtook me on opening the carton that held my first online order of white rye flour and first clear flour. I built a sourdough starter from scratch—a process that prolonged my fevered anticipation by a couple of weeks—and, with bated breath, mixed my first rye dough, the Jewish deli rye recipe in Nancy Silverton's *Breads from the La Brea Bakery*.

It's not as though I came to the experience unprepared; I'd baked my first bread—really just shaped and put in the oven a piece of dough my grandmother gave me—before I reached school age. The joy of that experience never left me: in graduate school, living in a hippie co-op, I turned out loaves by the dozen, perfuming the former fraternity house once or twice a week with the ineffable aroma of baking bread. But come graduation, the imperatives of career, marriage, and family drew me in other directions. It was only in the late 1990s, after my children were grown and my career was winding down, that I decided to bury my hands in dough once more. A decade later, attempting my first rye bread, I still felt like a rank novice.

That rye dough was everything I expected—sticky, dense, unwieldy. I'd never worked with rye before and was unfamiliar with how rapidly it would rise. As it turned out, I erred on the side of caution, put the breads in the oven too early, and was rewarded with blown loaves, their sides torn open by the explosion of steam that happens when underproofed dough meets high heat. Even so, that first effort, flawed as it was, was ambrosial; I finished half a loaf at one sitting. The taste and texture I'd been craving for so many years were now within my power to re-create.

It was a watershed moment.

My experience with rye grew while I worked on *Inside the Jewish Bakery*, a book I wrote in 2010 to tell the story of the Jewish bakeries that were an integral part of the Brooklyn neighborhood where I spent my childhood. To be sure, traditional Jewish rye breads occupy an important place in that book. But in the course of my research I also encountered a deeper layer of rye baking, which until then lay outside my experience—the dense, intensely flavored black breads that sustained my grandparents and their grandparents in the villages and towns of Eastern Europe. I wanted to know more about the breads that came to America but had already disappeared from Jewish bakeries by the end of World War II: as immigrant memoirist Harry Roskolenko puts it, "the various breads of the world, Russian, Polish, Hungarian, Austrian, German—all heavy, all good."[2]

And so I began in earnest my exploration of the world of rye. My Internet search efforts yielded a handful of recipes in English, many of which struck me as deliberately compromised so as to accommodate American home bakers, American groceries, and American tastes. But I wanted the real deal. With the help of some translation and unit conversion software, along with my own foreign language abilities, I began exploring blogs and recipe sites from the world's preeminent rye bread regions—Scandinavia, the Low Countries, France, Germany, the Baltics, Poland, Russia. There were some surprises, such as my discovery of a rye tradition in the mountainous Trás-os-Montes region of northwestern Portugal and of the rich rye baking culture of Trentino-Alto Adige (South Tyrol), nestled in the Alps of northeastern Italy. I began accumulating baking books in French, German, Russian, and Polish. And I explored the scholarly literature on rye's history, chemistry, and cultivation.

Over time I accumulated—and baked—a couple hundred recipes, representing the world's rye cultures and traditions. I fell in love with their tastes and textures and came to accept as the price of admission, and even look forward to, the tenaciously sticky, temperamental doughs I knew awaited me. I wondered at rye's many faces and flavors, from the rustic French *pains de seigle* and Dutch *roggebroods* to the rich, deep black pumpernickel of Westphalia, the thin, crackly *knäckebröds* of Scandinavia, anise-fennel fragrant Swedish *limpas*, and the extraordinary diversity of rye breads from Germany, the Baltics, Poland, and Russia.

Baking those traditional European and American rye breads led me to experience, both intellectually and through all my senses, the challenges of rye and the methods that bakers developed over centuries to tame the recalcitrant grain. It taught me patience and opened my eyes and my mind to techniques and possibilities I could barely imagine before that first blown loaf launched me on my journey. I don't know that I could, or would, want ever to go back to living without rye.

THE UNRULY WEED

Rye's role in the history of Europe is large—and largely overlooked. It was rye that fed Geoffrey Chaucer's London and François Villon's Paris, rye that fueled the empires of Charlemagne and Peter the Great, and rye that filled the ships of the Hanseatic League—the vast medieval mercantile federation that for four centuries united the nations of the North and Baltic Seas. And it was rye that sustained the first Europeans as they settled in North America.

Of course it was not always so. Rye first appears in the archaeological record about 13,000 years ago, in the area surrounding Mt. Ararat in eastern Turkey. From there, historians say, it followed the Euphrates River southward, into the Fertile Crescent, to settlements called Mureybet, Abu Hureyra, and Jerf el Ahmar.[3] The evidence is scant—a few charred grains and clay impressions of what is unmistakably wild rye among much larger troves of barley and the primitive wheat called einkorn, suggesting that during those early years rye entered the human diet as a stowaway, a humble weed hidden among the harvest.[4]

Then something very interesting happened—something that foretold the weed's future. About 12,000 years ago, Earth entered a period of global cooling that academics call the Younger Dryas, aka "the Big Freeze." Along with the rest of our planet, the Fertile Crescent turned dry and cold. Barley and einkorn struggled in those conditions, but rye flourished. And so the farmers followed the path of least resistance—and greatest yield. For 1,300 years, the abundance of domesticated rye in ancient grain troves attests not only to its importance in the human diet[5] but also to its newly recognized standing as one of the founder crops in the Near East.[6]

But rye's moment in the prehistoric limelight was not to last. The Big Freeze waned, Earth warmed, and barley and einkorn regained their dietary preeminence. For the next five millennia, rye surfaced only sporadically in the Fertile Crescent: around ninety-four hundred years ago at Can Hasan III,[7] five thousand years later at a Turkish Bronze Age site called Alaca Höyük,[8] and about four thousand years ago at Shahr-i Sokhta in modern Iran.[9] After that, rye disappears from the Near Eastern archaeological record.

It found a new home in central Europe. More than 6,000 years ago, rye appeared as a wild grain in modern Greece, the former Yugoslavia, and Ukraine.[10] Cultivated rye first appears in what is now Poland[11] and Bulgaria,[12] brought there by farmers who migrated from the Middle Danube region.[13] It flourished in the region's clay and acidic sandy soils, as well as its dry, cold climate.

Unlike wheat, millet, and barley, rye withstood drought conditions, germinated at temperatures near freezing, and resisted winterkill even at forty below zero.[14] And so throughout its new environment, rye prevailed over wheat, oats, and barley—just as it had in the Fertile Crescent during the Big Freeze.

Rye cultivation continued to spread across Europe during the pre-Roman Iron Age and was a staple grain during Roman times. At the height of the empire, it was grown widely to the north and east, but hardly loved. Pliny the Elder (AD 23–79), wrote in his *Historia Naturalis* that it "is a very poor food and only serves to avert starvation" and is mixed with wheat "to mitigate its bitter taste, and even then is most unpleasant to the stomach." A century later the Roman physician-philosopher Galen of Pergamon (AD 129–216), having tasted rye in the Balkans, dismissed it as barely edible because of its black color and bad smell.[15]

Rye benefited from two important technological advances that drove the rapid expansion of European agriculture between 500 BC and AD 1000—widespread adoption of the iron sickle and the appearance of the heavy plow.

Until the Iron Age, farmers had harvested their grain crops ear by ear, choosing only the more desirable cereals, typically wheat and barley, leaving weeds like rye for the birds and rodents. The practice made for inefficient but highly selective harvesting, conferring an artificial advantage to grains preferred for their look and taste.

With the iron sickle, farmers could clear-cut their fields close to the ground, which was more efficient but far less selective, collecting in the process weeds like rye along with the more desirable grains. Over time, as farmers replanted part of their harvest, the proportion of rye naturally increased in places where marginal conditions favored its growth. Indeed, experiments conducted after World War II in the region surrounding Berlin showed that within a period of three years rye completely took over self-seeded fields initially planted half wheat and half rye.[16]

The heavy plow further cemented rye's presence in the grain fields. Unlike its predecessor, the scratch plow—a rudimentary tool well suited to powdering the topmost layers of light Mediterranean soils—the heavy iron plow dug deep into the dense clay soils of northern Europe, improving drainage and bringing nutrient-rich subsoil layers to the surface.

The new plow also changed patterns of land use. Under the three-field system, which had prevailed since the time of Charlemagne, farmers planted one-third of their land in winter wheat or rye, another third in spring and summer crops, and left the remaining third fallow. Heavy plowing let farmers in coastal Holland, Germany, and southern Scandinavia manure intensively and sow rye in the same fields year after year.[17] In the Nordic countries, the new implement let farmers clear land for rye cultivation by burning the dense pine forests and then plowing the ashes under.[18]

The rapid growth of rye cultivation during the High Middle Ages increased the food supply and encouraged migration into formerly inhospitable regions of northern and central Europe. This, in turn, fueled the rise of social infrastructures that created the conditions for massive population growth. In the mid-seventh century, it's estimated that Europe's population was stable at around 18 million. By AD 1000, it had more than doubled to 38.5 million and then doubled again to an estimated 73.5 million in 1340, a decade before the Black Death of 1348–50 claimed the lives of half that number. Tellingly, most of this growth occurred in the rye-growing regions.[19]

Throughout the premodern period, bread was the foundation of the European diet at every level of society. On average adults consumed nearly three pounds of bread and gruel daily, which comprised about three-quarters of their caloric intake.[20] And while wheat may have occupied the top of the grain hierarchy, in large part because of its light color and relative scarcity north of the Alps, it was rye that fed the masses. In the view of medieval physicians, pure white leavened bread possessed special curative powers[21] and, as the standard of excellence, was reserved largely for the tables of the nobility and their ecclesiastical peers. Peasants and tradesmen, on the other hand, made do with dark whole-grain breads or breads made of a wheat-rye blend called maslin in Britain and *méteil* in France. Even today the social distinctions implicit in white and dark bread survive in the Breton expression "to finish eating one's black bread" (*finir de manger son pain noir*), which describes the return to comfort after a period of hardship.

From the Renaissance to the Industrial Revolution, rye prevailed across Europe's northern tier. In the seventeenth century it grew widely in the British Isles and covered half of all the cultivated land in Russia.[22] Finland emerged as an important producer and exporter into the Nordic region, sending its rye to Sweden, Estonia, Lithuania, and Russia—and from there via Hanseatic traders to Holland, England, Portugal, and Norway.[23] As late as 1908, rye-centric diets sustained an estimated one-third of Europe's population west of the Urals.[24]

Rye came to the New World in the early 1620s, carried there by British and Dutch colonists who planted it from Nova Scotia to Virginia. As in Europe, rye quickly became a prized commodity: in 1637 a bushel of rye on the New Amsterdam market brought the 2012 equivalent of $17.30, while in 2012 that same bushel fetched only $7.69. Wheat, on the other hand, figured only slightly in the diet of the first colonists; it was rye and native maize that nourished America during its first 200 years of settlement and westward expansion.

But rye's primacy was not to last. The opening of the western plains and the introduction of mechanized agriculture in the mid-nineteenth century—spurred on by Cyrus McCormick's 1834 patent for the world's first mechanical reaper—inundated North America with an ocean of wheat that all but swept rye out of the American diet. To fuel its Manifest Destiny as a nation that spanned the continent, the U.S. government gave away millions of acres of rich prairie land, much of it quickly planted to wheat. In 1866, American wheat farmers harvested a total of 15.4 million acres; by 1900, that had more than tripled to 49.2 million acres, and in 1948, wheat acreage peaked at nearly 76 million.[25] The railroads quickly followed, crisscrossing the Great Plains and providing the infrastructure that not only moved the wheat from farm to market but also, in doing so, became the midwives of America's global economic primacy.

By the turn of the twentieth century, wheat had conquered America; now foreign markets clamored for as much as U.S. farmers could provide. The taste of wheat, along with its social cachet, continued to hold sway in Europe, as it had since the Middle Ages. In 1866 the United States exported six million bushels of wheat, amounting to about 2% of its total harvest. In 1900 exports rose to 102 million bushels, or about 15%, and by the latter half of the twentieth century the United States was selling more than 1 billion bushels annually, fully one-third of its total wheat crop, to foreign buyers.[26]

Technology abetted the wheat juggernaut's inexorable spread as selective breeding programs spawned hardier and more prolific strains able to thrive in soils and conditions that once supported only rye. The Green Revolution of the 1950s and 1960s, with its emphasis on high-yielding varieties of wheat, corn, and rice, expanded wheat's share of global farm output even further, driving

rye back into the margins of food cultures it once dominated.

Since the latter half of the twentieth century, this change has been most apparent among the world's great grain nations. Between 1961 and 1991 rye harvests in the world's top three producers, the former USSR, Poland, and Germany, fell by 2.3%, 29.4%, and 17.3% respectively, while their wheat harvests grew by 15% in the USSR, 232% in Poland, and a staggering 560% in Germany. From more than nine million metric tons in 1992, the Russian Federation's rye harvest fell to just over two million metric tons in 2011—a drop of nearly 80%—while its wheat crop grew from forty-six million metric tons to fifty-six million metric tons. Even in Finland, where it gets so cold that yeast can barely survive, rye production fell by 40% between 1961 and 2011, while wheat more than doubled.[27]

In the United States, the decline was even more dramatic. In 1839, U.S. farmers produced nearly sixty-three pounds of rye for every American, falling to forty pounds per person in 1866 and less than twenty pounds in 1900. By the mid-1940s per-capita rye production dropped below ten pounds, and since 2010 it has hovered at just over one pound per person—much of it used for animal feed.[28]

For the populations of Europe's northern tier, rye has remained an enduring fixture of their tastes and traditions. In the United States, however, it's a different story: were it not for the rye-eating immigrants who swarmed into America until the Golden Door slammed shut in the late 1920s, rye would likely have retreated still further into history's shadows. Instead, German-inspired Milwaukee ryes, Nordic rye descendants, and Eastern European Jewish ryes and pumpernickels succeeded in winning permanent, if minor, places in America's culinary landscape.

THE REAPER'S HARVEST

But rye, unruly weed that it is, also has a dark side; for it was not only a bringer of life to the masses of northern, central, and eastern Europe but also, for nearly two millennia, of disease, madness, and death.

The primary culprit was a fungus called *Claviceps purpurea*, which attacks most

Ergots on rye head

cereals but has a special affinity for rye. Its spores, encapsulated in hard black kernels called *sclerotia*, winter in the ground until the coming of spring sets them free into flowering fields of rye. Borne on spring breezes, the spores parasitize the embryonic rye kernels in the same way that cowbirds insinuate their eggs into the nests of unsuspecting surrogates. The *sclerotium*-infected flowers secrete a sweet, sticky, spore-rich nectar that insects carry through the fields, producing a second wave of infection. The *sclerotia* mature on the ear as black, hornlike growths that resemble the sharp spurs on a rooster's feet—*ergots* in French.

During normal years, rye flowers for a few days at most, but in years when winter is cold and spring rainy—conditions that, before the twentieth century, were almost inevitably followed by famine—the rye blossoms can stay open for weeks, allowing the ergot to spread unhindered. For the rich, who could afford white flour even in times of scarcity, famine was a minor annoyance. The poor, who even in good times had to content themselves with flour adulterated with husks, sawdust, sand, and worse,[29] ate anything they could—even each other.[30] Bread made from the black grain was always preferable to no bread at all.

Ergot attacks on many fronts: its cocktail of potent toxins—including LSD's precursor, lysergic acid—affects the cardiovascular, gastrointestinal, reproductive, and central nervous systems. Symptoms can include convulsions, uncontrollable muscle spasms, hallucinations and bizarre behavior, gangrene and loss of limbs, blindness, deafness, suppression of fertility and miscarriage, and the sensation of intense burning or of insects burrowing under the skin.[31] By the tenth century, this feeling of unbearable, inexplicable heat earned ergotism the name "holy fire" (*ignis sacer*, *feu sacré*), which, by the 1200s, morphed into St. Anthony's fire, in honor of the saint whose order established hospitals to treat the affliction.

Between the sixth and eighteenth centuries annalists recorded no fewer than 132 large-scale outbreaks, primarily in France and Germany, but also as far south as Italy and as far north as Norway.[32] Mortality rates often exceeded 40%,[33] mainly among children and adolescents, who typically consume more food per unit of body weight than adults.

In France, the variant called gangrenous ergotism prevailed. Victims suffered hallucinations, delirium, sensations of intense burning, dry gangrene, and the loss of fingers, toes, or entire limbs.[34] In 857, for example, following a severe winter, "a great plague of swollen blisters consumed the people by a loathsome rot, so that their limbs were loosened and fell off before death."[35] In 945, "a plague of fire that burnt and gradually consumed limbs until death ended the torment"[36] broke out in Paris. The last confirmed outbreak in France occurred in the Rhône Valley south of Lyon in 1856.[37]

In Germany, the disease most often presented as convulsive ergotism, which subjected its victims to epileptic fits and the involuntary contraction of muscles and connective tissue. In 1085, "in the western part of Lorraine a great pestilence came that left many tortured and twisted by a contraction of the nerves; others succumbing to the holy fire that blackened their limbs like charcoal before they died in misery."[38] Five centuries later, in the Duchy of Lüneburg, not far from modern Hamburg, a "new and unheard of disease" caused its victims to feel unbearable heat, combined with paralysis and convulsions of the hands and feet that compressed and bent the fingers into a fist so tightly "that the strongest man could not unbend them."[39]

Five centuries of global cooling starting in the early 1300s, and known as the "Little Ice Age," brought year after year of cold winters and rainy summers—and with them repeated outbreaks of ergotism.[40] According to some historians, ergot poisoning was the cause of the well-documented outbreaks of "dancing mania" that occurred in Aachen (1374) and Strasbourg (1518). There victims danced with manic abandon on bloody and lacerated feet, unable to stop themselves for days, weeks, and months, screaming in agony at the terrible visions that flashed before their minds' eyes.[41] Some survived; many died. The accounts agree that both events followed cold, rainy spring weather and years of poor harvests.

The princes of the Church regarded the calamities that fell upon the Late Middle Ages as punishments from God for the iniquity of the people,[42] and, for Church and laity alike, the logical leap between divine retribution and demonic possession was a short one. Starting in the fifteenth century and lasting until the mid-eighteenth century, an orgy of witch-hunting, persecution, and mass execution overtook Europe.

Today, with the luxuries of hindsight and scientific knowledge, it's not surprising that the regions most closely associated with witch-hunting and demonic possession also experienced frequent outbreaks of ergotism.[43] In Trier, for example, a rash of trials took place between 1580 and 1599, a period that coincided with the failure of all but two harvests; and in Ellwangen between 1611 and 1618, following abnormally cold winters and repeated crop failures.[44]

The usual targets, often chosen for reasons of social, economic, or personal vendetta, faced accusations that they used spells and magic to cause demonic possession, whose signs—fits and convulsions, hallucinations, extreme physical contortions that exhibited superhuman strength, odd facial expressions, personality changes, and unintelligible ranting—applied equally well to the symptoms of ergotism.

Historians continue to debate whether ergot played a role in the Salem witch trials of 1691–92—a theory first advanced in 1976.[45] What is known is that the girls at the center of the witch hunt exhibited the classic symptoms of possession. In the words of eyewitness John Hale, they were:

> . . . bitten and pinched by invisible agents; their arms, necks, and backs turned this way and that way, and turned back again, so as it was impossible for them to do of themselves, and beyond the power of any Epileptick Fits, or natural Disease to effect. Sometimes they were taken dumb, their mouths flopped, their throats choked, their limbs wracked and tormented.[46]

There is an equally strong case that claims *Claviceps* had nothing to do with the witch trials but that the girls faked their symptoms. According to eyewitness Thomas Brattle, "[m]any of these afflicted persons, who have scores of strange fits in a day, yet in the intervals of time are hale and hearty, robust and lusty, as tho' nothing had afflicted them."[47] In the absence of conclusive evidence one way or the other, the debate continues.

By the mid-1700s, witch mania subsided and advances in medicine and the natural sciences established a clear causality between *Claviceps* and its devastating effects. Even so, ergot poisoning was not recognized as a disease until 1853, which perhaps explains its continuing prevalence in Germany, France, and elsewhere until the late nineteenth century, especially in isolated rural areas that had limited contact with cities and centers of learning, where knowledge was more current.

Over the past century a wide range of mechanical and biological measures, including crop rotation, deep seeding, and insect and weed control, have reduced *Claviceps* to a minor agricultural problem, while strict government guidelines and refinements in milling technology, such as heat-drying and brine flotation, have virtually eliminated ergot contamination in our food supply. And although I occasionally come across random *sclerotia* in bags of malted rye produced in Germany, their scarcity attests to the effectiveness of modern farming and processing methods:

Ergots in malted rye

I know that I can eat a Reuben sandwich or bake a loaf of pumpernickel secure in the knowledge that they hold no greater danger than perhaps a bout of indigestion.

RYE BAKING TODAY

White and black bread are the shibboleth, the call to battle, between Germans and French.

—Johann Wolfgang von Goethe[48]

There is a vast difference—perhaps reflective of broader, ages-old cultural tensions—between the wheat breads of France, which are the yardstick by most contemporary "artisan" baking is measured, and the rye breads of northern, central, and eastern Europe. Both bread cultures are deeply rooted in their birthplaces, and both continue to flourish. Only in America have we largely forgotten our culinary roots.

With a few exceptions—notably rustic breads like the celebrated *miches* of the Poilâne bakery, the rye-centric *méteils* and *pains de seigle* of Brittany, Normandy, and the Auvergne—the vast majority of French breads, and therefore, the American "artisan" breads that take French baking as their paradigm, start with refined wheat flour, water, salt, and yeast. Upon this foundation rests a superstructure of technique, so that a baker's skill is measured by the quality of his crumb and crust and her facility in creating the myriad of shapes—*baguettes, boules, bâtards, miches, couronnes, tabatiers, épis, fougasses,* and many others—that identify a bread's provenance.

In the rye world, shaping technique and the love affair with refined wheat flour take a backseat to flavor and texture. The breads are made of sourdough and whole grains, not only wheat and rye, but also spelt, oats, barley, and buckwheat. The bakers of rye extend their doughs with potatoes, cabbage both fresh and fermented, carrots, pumpkin, and/or other vegetables. To enhance flavor and texture and to provide that most precious nutritional commodity, fat, they may add tree nuts or perhaps the seeds of pumpkin, sunflower, flax, sesame, and poppy. For flavor they might perfume their doughs with anise, fennel, caraway, coriander, cumin and dill seeds, fresh and dried ginger, orange zest, or with the blue fenugreek that grows wild in Alpine meadows. For sweetness, their breads might incorporate dried fruit, honey, cane syrup, molasses made from sugarcane or sugar beets; or they might fortify their loaves with cured meats and dairy products like milk, cheese, buttermilk, yogurt, eggs, and butter.

To this myriad of ingredients the rye bakers add layers of method—the composition and grind of their flours, which can range from fine to barely broken; fermenting and mixing techniques; the use of small amounts of commercial yeast to give their soured doughs added lift; preferments and predoughs; and baking times and temperatures that are the legacy of the wood-fired ovens that once baked all of Europe's bread.

Those origins—the bread's *terroir*—continue to express themselves in the diversity of the world's rye breads. The more I read about rye's history and experienced its many iterations in my own kitchen, the more clearly I saw how each region's geography, climate, native flora, agriculture, and economics influenced its breads, endowing them with distinctive personalities. I grew to understand and appreciate the incredibly sophisticated techniques that European bakers developed—largely through trial and error—to control rye's unruly chemistry and coax the last iota of flavor from the refractory kernel.

In the far North, where yeast struggled to survive the bitter winter cold, baking took place twice a year and lasted for weeks, yielding hundreds of barely leavened rye crispbreads and rock-hard circular loaves with holes in the center for storage on poles hung from the ceiling. In southern Scandinavia, the Baltics, and northern Germany, buttermilk and yogurt soured the bread, and where barley grew the bread often contained beer. In the northern coastal regions, the bread was sweetened with honey and perfumed with anise, dill, and fennel. To the east, in Russia and what is today northern Poland, the breads were dark, sour, and pungent with cumin, caraway, and coriander.

Across rye's southern tier, the breads—typically rye blended with wheat or spelt—were lighter in color and finer in texture. In southern Poland and Ukraine, light-colored breads prevailed, often made with soured milk, potatoes, cumin, caraway, and astringent black caraway (nigella) seeds. In Alpine Austria and Italy, the breads and rolls bore the sweet, earthy fragrance of anise, fennel, and wild blue fenugreek. In the mountains of Auvergne and Provence, and in the Galicia region of Spain and the Trás-os-Montes region of northeastern Portugal, rye flour was simply substituted for wheat flour in plain loaves made only of flour, water, yeast, and salt. And in bread-loving Germany, with its diverse geographies and regional cultures, a myriad of rye breads ran the gamut of flavors, textures, and ingredients.

Rye baking in Europe is alive and well. In northern and eastern Europe, rye bread is more than a daily staple; it's both symbol and source of national identity—and something that's sorely missed when northern Europeans find themselves expatriated, or even on extended vacation.[49] Blogs, bulletin boards, and recipe sites devoted to bread baking abound, with rye bread recipes well represented. In Germany, books like *Deutschlands bester Bäcker* (Germany's Best Bakers) and *BROT: So backen unsere besten Bäcker* (BREAD: This Is How Our Best Bakers Bake) celebrate rye breads, while innovators like Germany's Peter Kapp and

Wolfgang Süpke and Sweden's Johan Sörberg enjoy near celebrity status.

In the United States, rye baking is on the cusp of a renaissance. At the turn of the twenty-first century a decent loaf was almost impossible to find outside of Eastern European neighborhoods—and, frankly, some of the best commercial rye breads are still to be found there. And although the focus of America's craft baking community still centers squarely on the wheat hearth breads of France and Italy, more and more American bakers are adding rye to their repertoires—and not just classic American light ryes, but the high-percentage traditional rye breads of western Finland, Latvia, Germany, and France. "When you bite into a dense, delectable slice," rhapsodized *New York Times* journalist R. W. Apple, "you have a sense that you are eating something primeval, something undying, something expressive of its origins, like honest wine."[50]

For decades rye has been one of America's best-kept and undeservedly obscure culinary secrets, and I rejoice that others have begun discovering its joys. For rye is more than just a strong-tasting, dark, unruly bread grain: it's also a piece of our collective history that's been overlooked and underappreciated for far too long.

Unlike wheat flours, which are virtually indistinguishable by sight, rye flours come in several distinctive varieties. Counterclockwise from the top: **white rye flour**, **medium rye flour**, **dark rye flour**, **fine rye meal**, **medium rye meal**, **coarse rye meal**; in the center, **malted rye berries**.

Ingredients

I CAME to rye baking with a relatively firm grasp of the behavior and chemistry of wheat flours. After much reading and experimentation I began to understand the effects of a flour's protein and ash content on both dough behavior and the taste, texture, and appearance of finished products. I delved into the mysteries of gluten formation and how mixing and kneading technique influence the character of the crumb. And I learned how to use time and temperature to manage yeast and enzyme activity to coax as much flavor as possible out of my doughs.

Then I met rye, and my baking gestalt went, if not upside down, then certainly several degrees off kilter. It was only after a few very frustrating weeks and many less-than-successful loaves that I learned my first and most difficult lesson: to master the mysteries of rye, I had to pretty much forget everything I knew about baking wheat breads, because rye's chemistry dictates an entirely different set of rules.

FLOUR

Without flour, there is no bread. And while that may seem excruciatingly obvious, the fact is that without a firm understanding of flour composition and chemistry, few, if any, bakers can hope to take their breads to the highest possible level.

Broadly speaking, a cereal kernel—be it wheat, rye, barley, oats, whatever—consists of four distinct zones: the bran, the endosperm, the aleurone layer—itself a complex of many layers—and the germ. The sections vary in function and nutritional value, and their proportions in flour affect a dough's baking quality as well as the flavor, aroma, and texture of baked goods. The following percentages are approximate values; the actual proportions vary from species to species, grain to grain, and even from one field or harvest to the next, depending on growing conditions.

- The **bran** is the coating of the kernel—rich in fiber (40%), protein (15%), and fat (10%)—that maintains its integrity until germination and the swelling of the endosperm cause it to split.

- The **endosperm** consists of about 75% carbohydrates, 8% protein, and less than 1% fiber. Its purpose is to provide nutrients, in the form of sugars, to the plant embryo upon germination. The bulk of the flour we use consists of this energy-rich, starchy endosperm.

- The **aleurone layer**, only a few cells thick, lies between the bran and the endosperm. It's rich in fat, fiber, and protein and provides a home for both the amylase enzymes that turn the endosperm starches into sugar and the lactic acid bacteria that regulate the germinated seed's acidity for optimal plant growth.

- The **germ** contains the plant's embryo, encased in a matrix of fat (10%), protein (23%), fiber (13%), and carbohydrates (51%).

Think of it this way: if a grain of wheat or rye were an egg—which indeed it resembles, structurally—the bran would be the shell, the aleurone layer the white, the endosperm the yolk, and the germ the embryo attached to the yolk.

For virtually all of our history, we humans have pounded, crushed, and ground grain into particles small enough to form a dough when they're mixed with water. Until the late nineteenth century we milled our grain between stones, whether they were Mesoamerican *metates,* African and the Near Eastern saddle querns, or the massive pairs of millstones powered by wind, water, and animals that supplied flour to the citizens of Rome and have persisted into modern times.

Those stone mills ground all parts of the kernel without distinction—bran, aleurone layer, germ, and endosperm—as well as significant amounts of husk, dust, pebbles, soil, rodent waste, and insect fragments that accidentally or deliberately found their way into premodern bread. To get white flour, the millers sifted the milled grain, a process called bolting.

Around 1870, however, milling technology was catapulted forward by the introduction of steel or porcelain rollers called *breakers*. Where the bottom stone of the old mills remained stationary while the upper stone rotated at a single speed on a vertical axis, the breakers rotated on horizontal axles and could be set to revolve at different speeds, different directions, and different distances from each other. This enabled them not only to strip away the bran and germ but also to extract fragments of varying size and density from the endosperm and its aleurone wrapper. The new technology gave millers the ability to isolate different parts of the kernel by "breaking" the same grains multiple times, making incremental adjustments of speed and spacing to produce specific results. Thus in a modern flour mill, the first set of rollers has the widest gap and gently crushes the grain, loosening the bran and germ and crushing out the finest, starchiest portions of the endosperm. After that first breaking, sifters sort the fragments by size and blowers sort them by weight. The bran, germ, and the first flour go into separate holding bins, while larger pieces pass through additional sets of breakers, sifters, and blowers. At each stage the process generates more streams of flour, each representing a distinct part of the kernel, each with its own protein, fiber, fat, and starch content. In all a single kernel of grain passes through four or five pairs of rollers, as well as dozens of sifters and blowers, before it's transformed into flour. Millers blend the various streams into flours of consistent quality whose specifications fit their end use, whether it be cake and pastry, bread, pizza, bagels, or animal feed.

For home bakers and professionals alike, two components determine a given flour's use—protein content, which in wheat flours is an indicator of gluten strength, and ash content, which is a measure of a flour's fiber (determined by incinerating a fixed quantity of flour and weighing the residue). Ash content also indicates the intensity of a flour's flavor because fat, which is the most efficient flavor carrier, tends to concentrate in the high-fiber zones of the kernel: the germ, bran, and aleurone layer. For that reason whole-grain breads are invariably more flavorful than breads made with refined flour—it's also why whole-grain flours are more prone to rancidity than their refined siblings.

There's a close relationship between both components. Most of a kernel's protein and fiber content concentrates toward its surface, so that the higher a flour's protein content, the higher its ash content. In the United States, there are no official flour classifications, as there are in Europe, but in general U.S. millers and bakers use protein content as their yardstick, as the table on page 28 shows.

	TYPE	PROTEIN	ASH
Wheat Flour	Cake/Pastry	7.0–8.5%	0.35–0.40%
	All-Purpose (AP)	10.0–11.5%	0.45–0.50%
	Bread	12.0–13.0%	0.48–0.54%
	High-Gluten	13.5–14.5%	0.52–0.56%
	First Clear	14.0–16.0%	0.80–0.90%
	Whole wheat	13.4–14.0%	1.60–2.0%
Rye Flour	White	6.0–8.0%	0.65–0.70%
	Medium	9.0–11.0%	1.25–1.45%
	Whole-Grain	9.0–11.0%	1.35–1.65%
	Dark	12.0–14.0%	2.25–2.55%

Most of the flour types listed in the table are self-explanatory, except, perhaps for first clear flour, so here goes:

Among the wheat flours, first clear flour is what remains of the crushed and sifted hard wheat endosperm and aleurone layer after the finer all-purpose, bread, and high-gluten grades—called *patent flours*—have come out. Because of its high protein content and strong flavor, first clear flour most often is used in rye, barley, and oat breads, low- or nongluten-forming grains that need an extra lift to form a proper crumb.

Substitution: Since first clear flour can be hard to come by for home bakers, a high-gluten flour with protein content in the 13.5–14.5% range will work just as well—but that, too, may be hard to find. In that case, adding 9 g/0.35 oz./1 Tbs. of vital

wheat gluten (77% protein) to 260 g/9.2 oz./2 cups of bread flour or to 130 g/4.6 oz./1 cup of AP flour will yield a close approximation.

In Europe, flour classifications are much more stringent, and based on ash rather than protein content. Note that although the U.S. flours have a lower nominal ash content than their European cousins, their true ash content is generally higher. This is because U.S. flour is measured on a 14% moisture basis for wheat flours and about 12% for rye flours, whereas European flour is measured 100% dry. To get true equivalency, divide U.S. ash content by 0.86 for wheat flour and 0.88 for rye flour. For example, U.S. all-purpose flour has a nominal ash content of 0.45–0.50% (which would classify it as a cake flour in Europe), but a true equivalent ash content of 0.52–0.58%.

Here's a quick summary of U.S.–Europe equivalencies:[51]

	U.S.	ASH (0% MOISTURE)	PROTEIN	GERMANY	POLAND	AUSTRIA	FRANCE
Wheat Flour	Cake	0.00–0.50%	8.5–9.5%	405	450	W480	45
	All-Purpose	0.50–0.63%	10.5–11.5%	550	550		55
	Bread	0.64–0.75%	11–12.5%	812	650	W700	65
	Strong Bread/ High Gluten	0.75–0.90%	12–14%	812	750		80
	First Clear	0.91–1.20%	13–15%	1050	1050		110
	Whole-Grain	1.21–1.80%	13–14%	1600	1400	W1600	150
	Graham	1.61–2.00%	13–14%		1850		
Rye Flour	White	0.00–0.90%	6.5–7.5%	815	500	R500	70
		0.91–1.10%	7–8%	997	720	R960	85
		1.11–1.30%	8–9%	1150	1150		85
	Medium	1.31–1.60%	9–10%	1370	1400		130
	Whole-Grain	1.61–1.80%	9–10.5%	1740	2000		170
	Rye Meal	1.61–2.20%	11–12%	1800			
	Dark	2.00–3.00%	12–14%			R2500	

Note that two of the European rye flours—German types 997 and 1150—don't have a U.S. equivalent, and only Austrian type R2500 is equivalent to U.S. dark rye—which, like first clear wheat flour, is the leavings of milled rye after the lighter grades have been sifted out. For breads traditionally built on one of the intermediate flours, I specify a blend of U.S. rye flours that approximates the composition of the European flour.

The lower the ash content, the lighter a flour's color and flavor. To adjust a bread's flavor profile, step the rye flour up or down one grade. For type 997, use 70% white and 30% medium rye flour. For type 1150, use 35/65 white/medium and for whole rye, use 55/45 medium/dark.

Common (and Uncommon) Flour Types

Besides rye and wheat, several other flours, grains, and grain products make cameo appearances in this book, notably:

- **Wheat bran** is exactly what its name describes: the fibrous outer coating of the wheat kernel. It's the same stuff that's used in bran muffins and bran breakfast cereals. In the rye world it shows up most frequently in breads from countries surrounding the North Sea, where its primary function is to lighten a rye bread's texture. This, by the way, is counterintuitive, especially among people who bake a lot of whole-grain and multigrain wheat breads. That's because bran makes wheat breads denser, rather than lighter, by literally cutting the gluten strands that support the crumb, limiting their ability to trap and hold baking gases. In rye breads, the bran, which is less dense than the heavy gels that form when rye meets water, lightens the dough without affecting its gas-trapping capacity, as in the Swedish "Archipelago" Bread (page 166). It's also great for dusting peels and coats the whole loaf of Slow-Baked Frisian Rye (page 155).

- **Spelt** is one of wheat's earliest ancestors, with a history of cultivation going back over six thousand years. At 17%, it's higher in protein than wheat, but far weaker in its ability to form gluten. Spelt grows best under conditions similar to wheat's, meaning that it requires a temperate climate and more fertile soils than rye. For that reason, spelt is far more common in the breads of the lower Alps and across southern Germany. Widely available in the United States, whole-spelt flour adds a sweet, nutty flavor to breads like Slow-Baked Finnish Rye (page 190) and Honey-Flaxseed Crispbread (page 169).

- **Barley** has been part of the human diet for at least ten thousand years. Like rye, it thrives in the marginal agricultural areas that abound throughout northern and eastern Europe; unlike rye, its weak gluten-forming proteins make it unsuitable for bread unless it's mixed with other flours or malted, as in East Berlin Malt Rye (page 145).

- **Oats** thrive in the cool, wet summers of northern and eastern Europe. Because of their high water absorbency and inability to form gluten, oats are generally used as a secondary bread grain, in combination with wheat and/or rye, such as in Salty Rye Rolls (page 141), and Mountain Oat Rye (page 295).

- **Buckwheat** is not a true grain but the seed of a fruit related to rhubarb and sorrel. It first appeared in the archaeological record about six thousand years ago and became a mainstay crop in the cold climate and acidic, nutrient-poor soils of northern Europe. Most often eaten by itself, buckwheat also appears in breads such as Slow-Baked Finnish Rye (page 190).

- **Maize** was the mainstay grain of the native Americans. The earliest European settlers in what is now New England quickly adapted it into their own diet. Rye and Indian Bread, a fifty-fifty combination of rye and cornmeal, was the staple food of the Massachusetts Bay Colony. Later, as European modes of agriculture took hold, the New Englanders enriched their Rye and Indian Bread with wheat, milk, and molasses, transforming it into the more refined Boston Brown Bread (page 91) that remains a Down East classic to this day.

LIQUIDS

The next most important element in a dough is the hydrating liquid. In most cases that's water, but many of the recipes also include whole milk, buttermilk, and yogurt, as well as beer and cider—foodstuffs that were integral to Europe's northern tier.

The meeting between flour and a liquid is where things really start to get interesting. The action all takes place at the molecular level, where chemical differences in rye and wheat drive contrasting reactions that quickly define the immense gulf between the two flours' behavior, treatment, and baking qualities.

To me wheat is simple and straight-forward—a steady, predictable flour that's cooperative and adaptable to many different ingredients, techniques, and end products. Rye, on the other hand, is complex and conflicted—not unlike the hubris-ridden protagonist of a Greek tragedy. On the path to becoming a proper loaf of bread, rye wavers between the poles of self-destruction and redemption, locked in an uneasy equilibrium until some outside force disturbs the balance.

That force is water.

When water meets wheat, two proteins, gliadin and glutenin, combine to form gluten, that stretchy, elastic stuff that makes possible paper-thin pizza crust, high-rise sandwich loaves, and the large-pored hearth breads that are the Holy Grail of artisan bakers. Gluten also does an admirable job of trapping the gases—mainly CO_2 and steam—released during fermentation and baking, then, as it cools, hardening into a flexible lattice on which hang the gelatinized starches that give wheat breads their texture and flavor.

When water meets rye, however, it unleashes a series of reactions that, if unchecked by the baker's steady hand, can result in anything from a paving brick to a gummy glob that grabs a bread knife the way a mucky swamp seizes a boot.

Rye proteins are weaker than wheat proteins and have only a very limited ability to form gluten, which means that rye breads can't depend on gluten to hold them together. Instead, rye contains an abundance of the complex carbohydrates called *arabinoxylans* that absorb large amounts of water, transforming those complex carbs into a dense, viscous gel. It's this starch-like gel that, like gluten in wheat breads, traps the fermentation and baking gases. However, unlike gluten, which continues to harden, causing wheat breads to turn stale quickly, rye's starchy gel structure remains tender long after baking, which is why rye breads stay fresh for weeks on end.

But there's a hitch. Rye, along with other grains, contains a group of enzymes, called *amylases*, that transform starches into simple sugars, a process called *amylase degradation*, aka "starch attack." Gluten is immune to amylase degradation. When I bake wheat breads, I can retard the dough, slowing its fermentation by cooling it overnight. Yeast activity slows as the dough cools, and the amylases convert wheat starches into sugar while the gluten structure maintains the dough's gas-holding ability.

In rye doughs, though, starch attack is a problem. Rye is far richer in natural sugars than wheat, and releasing them comes at a high price. Amylases are active at room temperature, so if rye dough stands for too long, the amylases can break down the starchy gels, robbing them of their ability to capture baking gases. But what's worse is that amylase activity spikes during the first minutes of baking, ending only when the dough temperature reaches 175°F/80°C and the enzymes become inert. At that point serious damage has been dealt to the bread. If left unimpeded, this starch attack will turn rye doughs into those dense, gummy loaves so frustratingly familiar to anyone who's ever baked with rye.

What is so intriguing about this biochemical drama raging inside the rye kernel is that within the problem lies the solution—in the form of lactic-acid-producing bacteria (LAB) that, along with wild yeast, live in the rye kernel's outer layers. The LAB work by turning simple sugars into lactic acid, the same stuff that gives yogurt, buttermilk, and sour cream their tang. Plus, depending on the dough's fermentation time and temperature and its flour-water ratio, LAB can also produce acetic acid, which gives vinegar its characteristic sharp acidity.

It's these acidifying effects of the LAB present in a healthy sour culture that allow rye doughs to hold fermentation and baking gases, since amylase activity drops to almost zero in acid environments, heading off the starch attack before it begins. In addition, the LAB also produce a natural antibiotic, cycloheximide, that kills off undesirable microorganisms but spares the yeast, which is why a healthy sour culture will never grow mold or go bad.

Temperature also matters. As the graph opposite illustrates, yeast and LAB activity peak at 82°F/27C° and 91°F/33C°, respectively, giving a theoretically ideal activity temperature—the point where the curves intersect—of 84°F/29C°. However, depending on the type of acid flavor and acid-yeast balance I'm looking for, these can change. Note, too, that although both yeast and LAB become nearly dormant at typical refrigerator temperatures, both continue to die off, producing alcohol in the process—something that brewers, distillers and vintners love, but not such a good thing for bakers, who rightly view a boozy sour culture as nutritionally challenged.

Given rye's chemistry, it makes perfect sense that the vast majority of the world's rye breads start with significant amounts of acidic, LAB-rich ingredients like yogurt, buttermilk, honey, fruit juices, vinegar, or a robust wild yeast, aka sour, culture.

Dairy products have historically been a major source of protein and fat, especially for the poor of Europe and the Middle East. Raw milk also carries LAB, which is what causes it to curdle and sour, eventually producing yogurt when left standing in a warm place. Butter, according to French annalist historian Fernand Braudel, was a luxury of northern Europe's elite that really didn't spread to the rest of the continent until the eighteenth century.[52] Even today butter shows up only rarely in European rye breads, and then primarily in the light breads of Scandinavia and southern Poland. Buttermilk, on the other hand, figures prominently not only in the breads of Scandinavia, Finland and northern Germany but also in the southern rye tier, from the Alps eastward to the Poland-Ukraine border regions.

Beer, like milk, has long been a part of the human diet and was the beverage of choice in places that couldn't support viniculture. In fact the German beer purity law, the Bavarian *Reinheitsgebot* of 1516, which provided that beer could contain malted barley, water, and hops only, came into being so that brewers wouldn't compete with bakers for wheat and rye, ensuring that bread remained affordable. Today beer is a key ingredient in the breads of the Nordic countries, northern Germany, and Bavaria—for example, Helsinki Buttermilk Rye (page 172), Ham and Dark Beer Rye (page 329), and Caraway Beer Bread (page 231).

Apples are a native of Spain that spread to southern France during the eleventh or twelfth century and then to Normandy five centuries later[53] before expanding into a global crop. Finnish Apple Bread (page 173) is a variation on Helsinki Buttermilk Rye

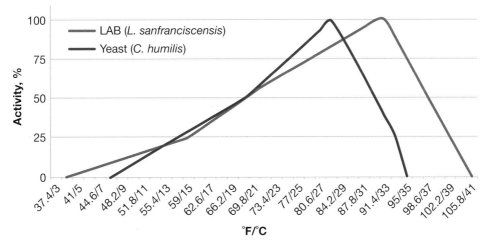

Temperature and LAB/Yeast Activity

Source: Gänzle, et.al., Appl. Environ. Microbiol. 1998, 64(7), 2616. at http://aem.asm.org/content/64/7/2616. Accessed 3/14/2014.

that substitutes unsweetened applesauce for a portion of the buttermilk. Apple cider, both hard and soft, appears in the breads of both Normandy and the Baltics, notably Normandy Apple Cider Rye (page 115) and Latvia's Sweet-Sour Rye Bread (page 250).

SALT

Salt is an indispensable ingredient in virtually all the foods we eat. Today we forget that salt was, at one time, a rare and costly commodity, often available only from state-sanctioned monopolies. According to Jeffrey Hamelman, bakers didn't start adding salt to their breads until the 1700s.[54]

Not only does salt contribute to flavor and baking behavior; it also inhibits yeast. Salt is hydrophilic—that is, water attracting—and so pulls water away from the yeast cells present in both doughs and predoughs, slowing its metabolism and rate of reproduction, while simultaneously increasing the sugars available for the LAB to metabolize into lactic acid. This chemistry in particular informs the Monheimer Salt Sponge technique (page 57), which calls for the addition of salt to a rye sponge to damp its leavening power while increasing its acidity. By increasing sugar content, salt also affects crust browning. Sugars brown more quickly than starches, so the higher the dough's sugar content, which is directly related to enzyme activity and inversely related to yeast activity, the more quickly and deeply it will brown.

The salt content of most wheat doughs is a fairly consistent 1.8–2.0% of total flour weight. The salt content of rye breads, meanwhile, can range from less than 1%, as in the Black Bread of Val d'Aosta (page 222), to the nearly 3% of Danish Rye Bread (page 127), depending on its provenance, percentage of rye flour, and other ingredients. On average, however, rye breads contain less salt than wheat breads, typically 1.6–1.8%.

LEAVENING

Leavening is the difference between a bread and a brick. The word itself comes from the Latin *libero*, which means "to raise," and is the ancestor of words like *levain* and *levadura* (French and Spanish respectively for leavening), *levitate, alleviate, liberate, libation,* and *lift*. Which makes perfect sense, considering that leavening is both the agent and the process that literally and figuratively elevates (also a *libero* descendant) the prosaic mixture of flour and water to a higher state of being.

WILD YEAST (SOURDOUGH)

Most of the rye breads in this book are built on wild yeast (sourdough) sponges, which not only leaven the loaves but also carry out the complex and necessary role of acidifying the dough against starch attack (see page 32). In many rye breads, in fact, it's the acid component of the sourdough that's more important than the leavening component. In those instances the sour sponge can ferment for up to 16, 18, even 20 hours, which weakens the yeast but greatly increases the acidity. To compensate for the loss of leavening power, rye bakers add a small amount of commercial yeast, a practice called "spiking" the dough.

HOW TO BUILD A RYE SOUR CULTURE
(The Case for Whole Grain)

It's not hard to make a rye sour culture from scratch; an online search will yield hundreds of recipes. Some use the wild yeasts that live on the skins of grapes, figs, and plums or "in the air"; others on the acid-producing bacteria present in buttermilk, yogurt, pineapple juice, raw onion, and a myriad of other acidic ingredients. Still others start with commercial yeast or store-bought starters. Fact is, none of these additives is necessary. All it really takes to build a delicious and robust rye sour culture is some whole-grain rye flour (preferably organic), water, a warm place, and patience.

All whole grains, and rye especially, contain an abundance of naturally occurring yeast and LAB, which, as described on page 32, are key to producing a good loaf. But there are other good reasons to build a sour culture on whole-grain rather than refined flours. First, the kernel's outer layers—the part that's been stripped away in refined flours—are rich in natural sugars, providing an immediate food source for the LAB and yeast. Second, and perhaps

A robust **rye sour culture** will show bubbles and triple in volume after fermenting for 8–10 hours at room temperature (68–72°F/20–22°C).

more important, their higher ash content creates a natural buffer that slows the acidification of the culture, allowing the LAB to produce acid for a longer time before high overall acidity slows LAB growth. This matters because final rye doughs contain lots of amylase-friendly starches and very little acid to control the enzyme's activity. By introducing high concentrations of lactic and acetic acid, a robust, well-buffered sponge immediately acidifies the final dough, inhibiting the enzymes and limiting the adverse effects of starch attack on the finished loaf.

STARTER SOUR (DAY 1)

INGREDIENT	GRAMS	OUNCES	VOLUME	BAKER'S PERCENTAGE
Whole-grain rye flour, preferably organic	70	2.50	½ cup	100%
Warm (105°F/41°C) water	70	2.50	¼ cup + 1½ tsp.	100%

1. Start with equal amounts of organic rye flour and water by weight, mix by hand into a stiff paste in a nonreactive (glass, porcelain, stainless-steel, plastic) container, cover, and let stand for 24 hours at room temperature (68–72°F/20–22°C) or slightly warmer.

NEW SOUR REFRESH (DAYS 2–7)

INGREDIENT	GRAMS	OUNCES	VOLUME	BAKER'S PERCENTAGE
Whole-rye flour, preferably organic	70	2.50	½ cup	100%
Warm (105°F/41°C) water	70	2.50	¼ cup + 1 Tbsp.	100%
Culture from preceding day	70	2.50	⅓ cup	100%

2. The next day, discard all but 70 grams of the culture and mix the remainder with the refresh ingredients, cover, and let stand. Repeat daily, discarding all but 70 grams of the preceding day's culture. After a week, the culture will be ready to use or to be stored refrigerated in an airtight container.

    The most important point to remember at the early stages is to feed the culture daily. Even when it shows no apparent fermentation, the yeast and

LAB are busy multiplying and consuming nutrients at a very high rate. By the second or third day, the sponge will swell, show bubbles, and give off a clean sour smell. Over the next few days the activity will become more and more vigorous and the smell more intense. Occasionally the yeast and LAB normally present in whole grains fail to establish themselves in a new culture; if, after 3 or 4 days, the culture darkens, develops a mold, or smells bad, dump the whole batch and start over.

Maintaining a Sour Culture

In a perfect world—or working bakery— sour cultures are refreshed daily. Jeffrey Hamelman recounted to me that when he was teaching at the Culinary Institute of America, his students' daily refreshed cultures consistently outperformed his, which

he fed thrice-weekly. "How chagrined I was," he recalls, "to see, time and again, that those ten-day-old cultures were making better bread than my twenty-year-old culture. It all came down to the feeding regimen."

That said, daily feedings demand both a degree of dedication and abundant flour supplies that are impractical for all but the most committed home bakers. Note, too, that many of the recipes in this book use sour sponges primarily as dough acidifiers and call for the addition of yeast to provide leavening power. For those breads especially, a culture that goes a few days between feedings will have larger, more robust LAB populations than those fed more frequently. For myself, refreshing once or twice a week strikes a happy medium—as long as I make sure to build my sponges on cultures that have never gone more than 36 hours since their last feeding.

MAINTENANCE REFRESH

INGREDIENT	GRAMS	OUNCES	VOLUME	BAKER'S PERCENTAGE
Medium or whole-grain rye flour	70	2.50	½ cup	100%
Warm (105°F/41°C) water	70	2.50	¼ cup + 1 Tbs.	100%
Rye sour culture	7	0.25	1½ tsp.	10%

Mix the refresh ingredients by hand until incorporated, cover, and ferment at room temperature (68–72°F/20–22°C) overnight, 10–12 hours. The sponge will be very bubbly, have a clean sour smell,

and will have tripled in volume. Store refrigerated in an airtight container and it will last indefinitely. My current sour culture, which I've had for about five years as of this writing, is built on a twelve-year-old sponge given to me by a friend in the Bay Area, who got it from another baker, who got it from another baker, and so on back into the distant past. Many European and U.S. bakeries—famously Orwasher's in New York City—boast sour cultures that are decades, if not centuries old.

COMMERCIAL YEAST

Commercial yeast, which arrived on the culinary scene during the nineteenth century, comes in three forms—fresh yeast (aka compressed yeast, cake yeast, and baker's yeast), which is a living colony embedded in a malt-based nutrient; active dry yeast, which requires rehydration before it's added to the dough; and instant dry yeast, which can go directly into the dough with no prior proofing. Bread machine or rapid rise yeast is instant dry yeast with added citric acid, an activity enhancer. Theoretically, all three forms provide equivalent leavening power: they consist of the same species, *Saccharomyces cerevisiae*—whose name, incidentally, reflects its beer ancestry—and they all inoculate the dough identically, by introducing the yeast spores into the flour-water nutrient mix. The difference, aside from the convenience of shelf life measured in years (for both types of dry yeast) or weeks (for fresh yeast), is that, in my experience, fresh yeast produces a more robust and even rise—due,

perhaps, to a higher concentration of live cells than the dry versions.

Functionally, all forms of yeast are interchangeable, but not gram for gram. Switching from one form to another is a simple matter of multiplying by the appropriate conversion factor, as shown in the table below. For example, if a recipe calls for 8 grams of instant yeast, multiply 8 grams by 2.5 (yielding 20 grams) to get the fresh yeast equivalent and by 1.25 (= 10 grams) for active dry yeast.

YEAST CONVERSION FACTORS
(multiply weight by)

to from	Fresh	Active Dry	Instant
Fresh		0.5	0.4
Active Dry	2.0		0.8
Instant	2.5	1.25	

CHEMICAL LEAVENING

Chemical leavening is based on one simple bit of chemistry: that an acid like vinegar, buttermilk, yogurt, honey, apple cider, or molasses combined with an alkaline (base) compound like baking soda, produces carbon dioxide. The CO_2, in turn, creates bubbles in a dough or batter that expand as they capture steam during baking, thereby raising the bread, pastry, or cake.

The first written reference to chemical leavening appeared in 1796, in *American Cookery*, by Amelia Simmons—generally regarded as the first American cookbook. In it the author calls for the addition of pearl ash, a mild form of lye derived from wood ashes, to gingerbread dough as a way of lightening the crumb. The technique soon spread across the Atlantic and by the mid-nineteenth century, bakers everywhere were leavening their quick breads, cakes, and pastries with some combination of acid and base. By the early twentieth century, sodium bicarbonate ($NaHCO_3$), aka baking soda, was the most widely used chemical leaven. Although most rye breads rely on yeast for leavening, a few, notably Boston Brown Bread (page 91), "Archipelago" Bread (page 166),

and Spiced Honey Rye (page 117) use baking soda.

Baking powder, which appears in a couple of the recipes, is simply baking soda with an acidifier built in. A British pharmacist, Alfred Bird, invented the first baking powder in 1843 by combining baking soda and cream of tartar, which starts consuming the bicarb as soon as water hits it. Problem was these single-acting baking powders could run out of steam, literally and figuratively, before the proteins in the dough set, resulting in fallen cakes and doorstop quick breads. So the chemists went back to their labs and came up with double-acting baking powders, which contain both moisture-activated and heat-activated acidifiers, deferring some of the acid production until baking. Frisian Gingerbread (page 148) and Rye Biscuits (page 174) both use baking powder to lighten their crumb.

SWEETENERS

Sweeteners not only add sweetness to a bread's flavor profile but also intensify yeast activity and promote faster and richer browning of the crust. Perhaps because of rye's strong taste, sweeteners are much more common in rye breads than in wheat breads. White granulated sugar plays only a minor role; instead the sweeteners I've encountered in European rye breads have strong and distinctive personalities of their own.

- **Honey** is one of the oldest known sweeteners, if not the oldest, in our diet. The earliest depictions of humans gathering honey date back at least ten thousand years to the Spider Cave in Valencia, Spain.[55] Traditionally honey was purely medicinal, but for at least a thousand years it's been loved for its own sweet sake. Honey can be either raw or pasteurized. Raw honey is usually cloudy and crystallizes if left standing; pasteurization, which kills the yeast present in raw honey, clarifies it and retards crystallization, but with some loss of flavor and aroma. To liquefy crystallized honey, microwave it for 30 seconds or immerse the container in hot water.

Depending on its nectar source, honey also can come in a variety of flavors and colors. Clover, acacia, and orange-blossom honey are pale and light flavored, with low acidity and flowery sweetness. Sage honey carries a spicy edge, while buckwheat honey is dark and highly acidic, with a trace of bitterness reminiscent of molasses. Wildflower honey and the blends sold at grocery stores offer a balance between sweetness and acidity. Choice of honey is a matter of taste; that said, I favor the robust flavors of buckwheat.

With an average pH of around 3.9, honey is highly acidic, making a perfect additive that not only slows starch attack (page 32) but also turns humble everyday loaves into extravagant celebration breads such as Spiced Honey Rye (page 117), Christmas Bread (page 257), and South Tyrolean Christmas Zelten (page 207); and toothsome small bites like Sunflower Seed Rolls (page 305) and Spiced Honey Squares (page 281).

- **Sugarcane syrups, aka light molasses,** come in several different forms. Cane syrup, a Louisiana specialty, is the boiled-down juice of sugarcane, while British golden syrup is a reconstituted syrup made of raw sugar and water, then filtered. Both cane syrup and golden syrup have very sweet flavor profiles, with little or no apparent acidity, and show up in many Nordic rye breads.

Unfortunately both cane and golden syrups can be hard to obtain locally, so I've found it useful to make a close equivalent out of water, unrefined sugar (turbinado or Mexican *piloncillo* or, in a pinch, dark brown sugar), dark molasses for flavor, and a touch of honey or corn syrup to prevent recrystallization.

INGREDIENT	GRAMS	OUNCES	VOLUME	BAKER'S PERCENTAGE
Raw sugar	260	9.15	1¼ cups	100.00%
Water	140	4.95	⅝ cup	53.85%
Dark molasses	21	0.75	1 Tbs.	8.08%
Honey or corn syrup	14	0.50	2 tsps.	5.38%

1. Combine the sugar, water, molasses, and honey or corn syrup in a saucepan. (If using *piloncillo*, which comes in a cone, pulverize it first with a hand grater or food mill.) Stir constantly over medium heat until the mixture reaches

230–235°F/106–112°C (thread stage on a candy thermometer).

2. Remove from the heat, strain through a fine sieve, and let cool. Will last indefinitely stored in a closed container at room temperature (68–72°F/20–22°C).

- **Molasses** is the juice of sugarcane or sugar beets that's been boiled down and some or most of the sucrose (white sugar), crystallized and extracted. Beet molasses (*Rübenkraut* or *Zuckerrüben-sirop*) comes in one grade, while sugar-cane molasses comes in three—light, dark, and blackstrap, each darker and more bitter than the preceding, with acidity increasing from about pH 5.6 to pH 4.9. Sulphured molasses is processed with sulfur dioxide, a bleaching and antimicrobial agent that can also leave an off taste. For that reason, I specify unsulphured molasses throughout. In general, the darker, heavier rye breads, such as GOST Borodinsky (page 253), Slow-Baked Frisian Rye (page 155), and Boston Brown Bread (page 91), use dark molasses, while milder-flavored Nordic and North German ryes call for either light molasses, malt syrup (see below), sugar beet molasses, or, in a pinch, dark corn syrup (pH 5.0–4.0).

- **Malt** is produced when a kernel of grain is allowed to germinate and then heat-dried to stop the process. Germination activates the amylase enzymes that transform starch into sugar, releasing the grain's natural sweetness. After germination has been stopped by drying, subsequent roasting caramelizes the sugars, allowing the malt to develop a range of flavor profiles from mild to pronounced.

The recipes in this book use two kinds of malted grain, rye and barley.

Barley malt, which comprises the raw material for most beers, is generally available through retail and online home brew outlets in a variety of roasts ranging from very pale to very, very dark. In the baker's pantry it usually takes the form of either dry or liquid malt extract or malt syrup, which is a blend of liquid malt extract and corn syrup. The recipe for East Berlin Malt Rye (page 145) is a rarity, since it features the malted grain and not the extract.

One point that deserves attention is whether the malt is diastatic—that is, contains an active amylase complex—or nondiastatic. Nondiastatic malts are used strictly to add the sugar maltose, which feeds both yeast and LAB and promotes browning, whereas diastatic malt increases the amylase enzymes present in a dough or predough (see page 32), accelerating the transformation of starch into sugar. The recipe for Belarusian Sweet Rye (page 277), illustrates the use of diastatic barley malt in predoughs.

Malted rye, which is used untoasted in Riga Rye (page 261), can also be found at home brew outlets. Many of the Russian and Baltic recipes, including Belarusian Sweet Rye (page 277), Scalded Rye

Bread (page 285), and GOST Borodinsky Rye (page 253) use red rye malt, which is malted rye that's either pan-roasted or oven-roasted until it's a red-brown color. The Ham and Dark Beer Rye (page 329) and Pumpkinseed Rye (page 131) use rye malt that's been toasted to a deep brown color, endowing it with a chocolaty, slightly burnt character.

Neither red nor black rye malt is easy to come by, so I end up making it myself by gently toasting brewer's malted rye in a skillet over medium heat until it turns fragrant and takes on, in the case of red rye malt, a deep rose pink color (3–4 minutes), or in the case or black rye malt, a deep brown (6–7 minutes). For larger quantities, I spread the malted rye on a sheet pan and roast in a preheated 450°F/230°C oven 15–18 minutes for red malt and 22–25 minutes for black.

Red rye malt

SPICES AND HERBS

There is a natural affinity between rye and spices, and virtually all of the spices used in European rye breads flourish in the cool temperate climates of the rye regions. The most commonly used rye spices—**anise, caraway, coriander, cumin, dill**, and **fennel**—are related to carrots, a hardy northern crop; only **nigella**, the acrid black seed called *czarnuszką* in Polish and *chernushka* in Russian, comes from south of the Alps.

In the North, anise, fennel, and dill perfume sweet rye breads like Swedish Sweet Limpa (page 185) and Lithuanian Christmas Bread (page 257), as well as savory Scandinavian crispbreads, which may also contain caraway. To the east, the bakers of the Baltics, Russia, and Poland favor the floral citrus of coriander and the bitter astringency of caraway, cumin, and nigella seeds. Throughout Germany, bakers use these spices not only individually but also in a blend called *brotgewürz* (bread spice) that combines the sweet fragrance of anise and fennel with the bitter astringency of caraway and the lemon notes of coriander.

Caraway comes to the fore in Old Milwaukee Rye (page 99) and German Caraway Beer Bread (page 231), while the unique aromatic spiciness of cumin has a prominent role in Cumin Rye (page 290), Lithuanian Spiced Honey Squares (page 281), and Poland's Zakopane Buttermilk Rye (page 299), which also features a topping of intensely flavored nigella seeds.

Dried orange peel, a product of the Mediterranean, probably first arrived along the coasts of the North Sea and Gulf of Finland in the hulls of the Hanseatic merchants who dominated northern European trade from the thirteenth to seventeenth centuries. It features prominently in Finland's Helsinki Buttermilk Rye (page 172) and Sweden's Gotland Rye (page 176) and also in some versions of Swedish limpa.

Holland, too, had its traders, seafarers who sailed across the tip of Africa to bring back the treasures of the East—**ginger, cinnamon, cardamom, cloves, mace,** and **nutmeg**—spices that add their flavors to Frisian Gingerbread (page 148), a holiday bread for which no expense is spared. The same rare spices—likely brought to the Italian Alps via Venice—also come to the fore in South Tyrolean Christmas Zelten (page 207).

German bread spice (*brotgewürz*) has no fixed formula but varies from baker to baker and region to region. The most common formulation—and the one I use throughout this book—calls for caraway, anise, fennel, and coriander in a 10-6-6-2 ratio. It's used extensively throughout Germany and takes center stage in Franconia Crusty Boule (page 239), Scorched-Crust Sour Rye (page 137), and Paderborn Rye (page 345).

In spring and summer, when they were in season, bakers added the bite and perfume of fresh herbs—parsley, dill, fennel, and chives—to breads like Dithmarsch Cabbage Rye (page 125) and the Swabian Rye Blossom (page 203)—the only two recipes in this book that use fresh herbs. Today, with fresh produce available year-round, I can enjoy those breads any time I like.

INGREDIENT	GRAMS	OUNCES	VOLUME	BAKER'S PERCENTAGE
Caraway seed	10	0.35	1½ Tbs.	100%
Anise seed	6	0.20	1 Tbs.	60%
Fennel seed	6	0.20	1 Tbs.	60%
Coriander seed	2	0.07	1 tsp.	20%

To make *brotgewürz*, toast the seeds in a skillet over medium heat, keeping them moving constantly, until they become fragrant, 2–3 minutes. Remove from the heat and let them cool, then use a spice grinder, blender, or mortar and pestle to grind to a fine powder. Stored in an airtight container, preferably in the freezer, it will remain fresh for 3–4 weeks.

Vinschgau Twins (page 244) uses the dried leaves of blue fenugreek (*brotklee* or *blauklee*), which grows wild in the Alpine meadows of South Tyrol.

OILSEEDS AND NUTS

More than the wheat breads I've baked and encountered, rye breads are rich in nuts and oilseeds, which contribute both their fat content and their distinctive flavors and textures. It's impossible to say whether bakers first included seeds in their bread for flavor or simply as a way to extend flour in years of poor harvest. No matter the reason, the seeds of flax, sunflower, and pumpkin—and, to a much lesser extent, sesame—provide fragrance, flavor, mouthfeel, and crunch to Europe's rye breads.

- **Flaxseed** has been part of the European diet for at least five thousand years, if not longer.[56] During the eighth century, Charlemagne promulgated laws that encouraged flax cultivation for both textiles and food.[57] Flaxseed is highly nutritious, containing over 40% fat, nearly 20% protein, and almost 30% fiber. Today it's used extensively in the breads of both the northern tier and the Alps—for example, Ammerland Black Bread (page 151), Danish Rye Bread (page 127), Black Bread of Val d'Aosta (page 222) and Honey-Flaxseed Crispbread (page 169).

- **Sunflower seeds**, a rich source of fat (over 50%) and protein (20%) are an American native that came to Europe in the sixteenth century via the Spanish. They quickly spread throughout the continent, where they became an important source of animal feed and, as seeds, meal, and oil, were incorporated into local and regional cuisines. Today sunflower seeds contribute flavor, texture, and mouthfeel to breads like Sunflower Seed Rolls (page 305), Rye Sticks (page 317), Hearty Seeded Rye (page 157), and Sauerland Black Bread (page 348).

- **Pumpkinseeds** are another New World ingredient that found its way back across the Atlantic not long after the first Europeans arrived in North America. I learned to love their sweet nuttiness as a kid, when my dad and I cleaned and roasted the seeds from our Halloween jack-o'-lantern. I fed my cravings at other times of the year with little boxes of massively salted pumpkinseeds I could buy at the candy store for a few cents. Like flax and sunflower seeds, pumpkinseeds are loaded with nutrition, consisting of 20% of a very fragrant, strong-flavored oil that's one of the hallmarks of eastern Austrian cuisine and nearly 20% each of protein and fiber. They have an especially prominent place in German rye breads, notably the Pumpkinseed Rye (page 131), and Weinheim Carrot Rye (page 321).

- **Sesame seeds** are an import from the Mediterranean that probably entered Europe during the Middle Ages via Venice, which was the trading portal for all of southern Europe, including the Transalpine region. Although their delicate flavor makes sesame seeds more suitable for wheat breads than for rye, they make appearances in rye breads from all across western Europe, including Italy's Black Bread of Val d'Aosta (page 222), and Swedish Honey-Flaxseed Crispbread (page 169).

Nuts, like oilseeds, add richness, flavor and textural notes to the rye breads of Europe. Unlike flaxseeds and pumpkinseeds, however, which are by-products of other primary crops, and sunflower seeds, which are the product of highly prolific annual plants, nuts are a primary tree crop with far more limited growing ranges than the plants that produce oilseeds.

- **Walnuts** and **hazelnuts** thrive in temperate climates and mountainous terrain. It's not surprising, then, that they show up in the Valais Rye (page 235) of Switzerland and in South Tyrolean Christmas Zelten (page 207), where they add textural surprises, as well as mouth-filling richness.

- **Almonds** and **pine nuts (*pignoli*)**, on the other hand, grow best in Mediterranean climates and contribute their sweet richness to South Tyrolean Christmas Zelten (page 207).

FRUITS, VEGETABLES, AND PROTEINS

There is a great and long-standing tradition throughout Europe of adding other foods to rye bread. Dried fruits traditionally were used to elevate the daily bread to mark special occasions—either life events such as births, christenings, and weddings, or religious observances, most notably Christmas. The Lithuanian Christmas Bread (page 257), Spiced Honey Rye (page 117), and South Tyrolean Christmas Zelten (page 207) all contain an abundance of dried and candied fruits, including **prunes**, **apricots**, **raisins**, **figs**, and **citrus peel**, none of which grew locally in Europe's rye regions and all of which, until the latter half of the twentieth century, were rare and precious indulgences. In Germany, the Baltics, and the Nordic countries, **apples**—fresh or cooked into applesauce—added moisture and flavor to the local breads.

Vegetables, on the other hand, were largely used to extend doughs, since a steady and affordable supply of flour often proved challenging for Europe's common folk. In some places they used whatever was easily available. In northern and eastern Finland, they extended their breads with flour made from the mildly toxic inner bark of pine trees; in Iceland, it was dulse, a kind of moss, that took the place of flour. The vegetables I've encountered in my exploration of rye have all been autumn crops that hold well over the winter—**potatoes**, **cabbage** (both fresh and fermented), **onions**, and **carrots** as in Lithuanian Potato Rye (page 283), Belarusian Sweet Rye (page 277), and Weinheim Carrot Rye (page 321), Dithmarsch Cabbage Rye (page 125), and Sauerkraut Bread (page 212), all from Germany.

From about the eighteenth century on, three-quarters of the average person's daily caloric intake came from cereals; they ate meat only a few times a year. For them, flour and water became the extender, carrying the flavor of those rare proteins into every bite, turning the prosaic into something special, as in breads like Ham and Dark Beer Rye (page 329) and Swabian Rye Blossom (page 203).

Dairy products were far more common and their consumption more widespread. Whole milk, yogurt, and buttermilk appear in rye breads across Europe. Polish Milk Rye (page 309) and Yogurt Rye (page 293), Helsinki Buttermilk Rye (page 172), and Münster Country Boule (page 325) are just a few examples.

STALE RYE BREAD

Only in rye baking have I encountered stale bread as a recurring ingredient. As a practical matter, bakers through the ages have recycled unsold bread, lost income otherwise, in a way that's largely undetectable. But too much of a good thing for bakers can be a bad thing for consumers: as a result, some countries have laws on the books limiting the amount of old bread in dough.

Chemically the gelatinized starches that make up the bulk of stale bread bind water far more effectively than raw flour, tightening the crumb of the finished loaves and reducing the notorious tendency of some rye breads to crumble at the slightest touch. Finland's Sour Ring Bread (page 181), Germany's Sauerland Black Bread (page 348), and the Austrian Country Boule (page 227), among others, all call for stale rye bread in their recipes. Since the percentage of old bread used in the recipes is so small—no more than 10% of the total flour weight—the type of bread really doesn't affect the flavor very much. I generally use leftover bread ends that I air-dry and keep in a plastic bag in my freezer.

Nine Steps to Great Rye Bread

BEFORE the age of science, with only experience to guide them, European bakers developed extraordinarily sophisticated ways of using time and temperature to harness the conflicting chemistries that come into play when rye meets water. When I first began experimenting with rye, I was more fortunate than those early bakers because I didn't have to reinvent any of their wheels. I did, however, have to learn techniques that, beyond creating a sourdough sponge, I'd never encountered during the years I spent baking wheat breads—nor had I ever been exposed to rye dough's challenging stickiness. Successes and failures not only deepened my understanding of baking temperature and the chemistries at work when water meets flour but gave me a new and powerful set of tools I could use to influence the tastes and textures of all my breads.

Generally speaking, all bread baking follows a similar path from flour and water to finished loaves; however, as the cliché goes, the devil is in the details—and there are plenty of details. Rye doughs are built on starchy arabinoxylan gels, not gluten, and so are highly susceptible to enzyme degradation, aka starch attack (see page 32), which can destroy the crumb. Even under the best of circumstances, rye's chemistry poses fermentation and proofing challenges that are absent in wheat breads and which mandate a set of different and often less forgiving process milestones.

Because they're built on starchy gels and not gluten, medium- and high-percentage rye breads require no extended kneading, resting, stretch-and-folding, or preshaping. On the other hand, because dough acidity is a rye baker's most powerful weapon against starch attack, the importance of starting with a robust sponge extends the baking timeline: where it normally takes me 8–10 hours to bake a sourdough wheat bread, start to finish, my rye breads typically require 16–24 hours—and sometimes longer—to go from raw ingredients to finished loaf. To simplify the time challenge, I include suggested starting times for each stage of recipes with more than 10–12 hours of preparation time.

If rye had a less fearsome reputation, I suspect many more people would be baking with it. Fact is, fermentation takes up most of the extra time, and the extra effort really centers on putting up with rye's stickiness and paying close attention to the loaves while they proof—not very onerous, but not very well understood. And when I consider the results in terms not only of the new flavors and textures but of the new understanding I've gained, rye has repaid many times over the extra time and effort it's demanded of me.

1. INGREDIENT PREPARATION AND MEASUREMENT

Before they do anything else, professional chefs and bakers make sure all their ingredients are arranged in front of them and ready to use, a practice called *mise en place* ("set in place"). I've learned through bitter experience that unless I lay everything out, the baking soda or sunflower seeds I was sure I had will be nowhere to be found, causing me unnecessary and frustrating delays.

The "ready to use" part of the equation is especially important because it pertains to any and all of the preparation—cutting, grating, precooking, toasting, grinding, and so on—that has to take place before the actual assembly and baking. Many of the recipes in this book call for that kind of advance preparation—for example, mincing, grating, and precooking the filling ingredients for Swabian Rye Blossom (page 203) and the cabbage and onions for the Dithmarsch Cabbage Rye (page 125); for toasting and grinding rye malt for Riga Rye (page 261) and bread spice (*brotgewürz*) for many of the German ryes. All of it needs to be done well beforehand and not at the last minute, when an extra 20 minutes of fermentation can ruin a loaf.

Accurate measurement is also important. Despite the fact that for over a century American cookbooks have used volume measurements—cups, tablespoons, and teaspoons—almost exclusively in their recipes, weighing is really the only way to ensure consistent results, especially in baking. That's because volume measurements ignore variations in density. Put another way, one cup of compacted flour can weigh 50% more than one cup of sifted flour, and a tablespoon of kosher salt, because of how it's manufactured, can weigh half as much as the same volume of table salt.

Back in the day when accurate scales were bulky and expensive and only merchants had them, recipes had to default to cups and spoons to make them accessible to home cooks. Today, however, that's not the case: the wide availability of inexpensive and highly accurate digital scales that read out in both grams and multiples of 0.05 oz. give us the ability to achieve a degree precision and consistency that was impossible not so long ago. (Note, however, that because of rounding, the ingredient and recipe weights given in the recipes that follow may not correspond exactly.) But not everyone is comfortable using a scale or has one. For that reason I've written the recipes not only in ounces and grams, but also in volume measurements taken from the weights given in the USDA Nutrient Database (http://fnic.nal.usda.gov/food-composition/usda-nutrient-data-laboratory).

I also provide baker's percentages using the conventions established by the Bread Bakers Guild of America (BBGA). The baker's percentage system expresses ingredient quantities as percentages of the total flour in a recipe. A basic baguette dough, for example, might be written as flour 100%, water 65%, salt 2%, instant yeast 0.8%, giving a total dough percentage of 167.8%. In practice, this means that a dough calling for 1,000 g of flour would use 650 g of water, 20 g of salt, and 8 g of yeast, for a total dough weight of 1,678 g, enough to make six baguettes weighing

about 280 g/10 oz. each before baking. I've given percentages for full recipes, to two decimal places, in the recipes themselves for straight doughs—recipes that have no intermediate stages between ingredients and final dough—and separately for recipes that have multiple stages.

Using baker's percentages isn't nearly as daunting as it may first appear. Since they remain constant for each bread, scaling recipes up and down becomes a matter of simple arithmetic based on how much flour I want to use or how much dough I need. Since metric measurements lend themselves much more readily to decimal calculation, I find it much easier to work in grams—which also, by the way, gives me much more precision when I measure, since $1 g = 0.0355$ oz., or two-thirds of the standard digital scale rounding unit of 0.05 oz.

To give an example, I remember developing a craving for pumpkin bread at a time of year when fresh pumpkins were out of season, so I had to use canned. Problem was, my recipe called for 500 g of pumpkin, while my can of pumpkin contained only 425 g, leaving me with the choice of opening a second can, which only changed my dilemma from one of deficit to one of surplus, or scaling the recipe down to fit the reality of the moment. Frugal baker that I am, I chose the latter. To find the percentage of pumpkin in one can versus the full recipe, I divided 425 by 500, which came to 85%. I then multiplied the weights of all the other ingredients by 0.85 and got the quantities I'd need for my scaled-down recipe. Needless to say, the bread turned out perfectly; I shudder when I think about doing that with ounces, let alone cups and spoons.

A second way baker's percentages are useful is when the amount of dough I want or need to make is different from the amount produced in the recipe. Suppose, for example, I need 10 baguettes, for a total of 2,800 g of dough instead of the 1,678 g I get using the quantities above. Again, by dividing 2,800 by 1,678—what I need versus what I know—I get 1.67 as the multiplication factor, which tells me that 1,669 g of flour will give me the amount of dough I need.

The recipes also include additional percentage information aimed at enhancing understanding of how the recipes work. Stand-alone percentages for the various predoughs show hydration and mixing ratios as if they were separate recipes—which, in a sense, they are. Following BBGA practice, I also give, where applicable, the percentage of prefermented flour, which affects the fermentation and proofing behavior of the final dough. Finally, percentages are not given for the final dough in multistage recipes because they can be misleading, especially for ingredients like salt and yeast, which, if measured incorrectly, can easily ruin a bread.

2. PREDOUGHS

More than any other type of baking, rye baking uses a wide variety of formulations that precede mixing of the final dough, which, for lack of a better term, I call *predoughs*. They include not only preferments—the sourdough and yeast sponges familiar to most professional and home craft bread bakers—but also soakers, scalds, and compound predoughs that I refer to as *scald-sponges* and *yeasted sour sponges*.

Preferments—Yeast and Sour Sponges

I think of growing a sponge as nothing short of miraculous: using a rye sour culture awash in enzymes and swarming with lactic acid bacteria (LAB) and yeast to inoculate a slurry of flour and water, transforming it, over hours or days, into a vast metropolis of living creatures. It's the metabolic by-products of those microorganisms—CO_2, lactic acid, and acetic acid—abetted by the enzymatic degradation of starch into sugar, that make bread possible.

For millennia, long before the advent of commercial yeast in the mid-nineteenth century, sponges leavened the breads of our ancestors. A robust sour sponge that contains at least 30% of a recipe's total flour virtually eliminates the need for additional yeast and produces both a well-developed crumb structure and complex flavor profiles that change from bread to bread.

It's not all that difficult to manage the acidity and leavening power of a sponge: think hydration and temperature.

Hydration of 80% or less and normal room temperature (68–70°F/20–21°C) favor yeast activity and, for longer fermentation times, acetic acid formation; sponges hydrated at 100%-plus and fermented at temperatures around 92°F/34°C have lower yeast activity and greater lactic acid content.[58]

Microbiologists who study sourdough fermentation classify sour cultures into four types,[59] shown in the table below.

	TYPE 0	TYPE I	TYPE II	TYPE III
Inoculant	Commercial yeast	Sour culture	Sour culture	LAB culture or sour culture
Flour	Wheat	Wheat/Rye	Rye	Wheat/Rye
Fermentation	3–24 hours	4–16 hours at 75–95°F/25–35°C	1–7 days at 82°F/28°C	—
Microorganisms	Yeast dominant, low LAB	Balanced LAB, yeast	LAB dominant	—
Final pH	3.5–5.0	3.5–4.0	3.2–3.8	—
Acidity	Low (<7)	Medium (5–20)	High (>20)	—
Suitability as seed culture	Not suitable	Suitable	Not suitable	Limited suitability
Function in baking	Leavening, improved flavor	Leavening, acidification	Acidification	Acidification

- **Type 0** sponges are the familiar poolishes, bigas, *pâtes fermentées* and *levains* that bring both leavening power and, more important, significant flavor improvement to craft wheat breads. They have no carryover value but are made as needed, using commercial yeast. In rye breads, Type 0 wheat sponges typically show up in combination with rye sponges and other pre-doughs, as in Vinschgau Twins (page 244), Franconia Crusty Boule (page 239), and Auvergne Rye-Wheat Boule (page 111).

- **Type I** sponges are the rye baker's workhorse, providing acidity, leavening power, and utility as a seed sour culture. As one-, two- and three-stage sponges (see below), they can ripen in both rye and wheat doughs, where the interaction of yeast, enzymes, and LAB create complex flavor profiles.

- **Type II** sponges ferment for extended periods, boosting their acidity to extremely high levels and creating environments that effectively kill off all but the most acid-tolerant microorganisms—mainly various species of LAB. They're used, either wet or in dried form, to acidify dough and, because of their *de minimis* yeast populations, are not suitable as seed cultures.

• As a practical matter, **Type III** sponges are pure LAB cultures and as such are used in dried form exclusively as acidifiers.

My workhorse rye sour culture is an 80–100% hydration Type I sponge that uses single-stage fermentation and 10% by flour weight of sour culture to inoculate the flour and water. It's a simple, dependable sponge that stood me in good stead as I baked my way through my collection of rye recipes. One lesson I've learned through bitter experience is to refresh my starter culture separately and no more than 36 hours in advance of bake day. That way I ensure that my culture is at peak vitality and also avoid repeating the time I used all of my starter culture for the recipe at hand, reducing me to scrounging the dregs that clung to my spatula and bowl to rebuild the culture.

Basic One-Stage Sponge (Hydration 80%–100%)

INGREDIENT	GRAMS	OUNCES	BAKER'S PERCENTAGE
Medium or whole-grain rye flour	70	2.50	100%
Warm (105°F/41°C) water	56–70	2.00–2.50	80–100%
Rye sour culture	7	0.25	10%

Mix the sponge ingredients by hand until incorporated, cover, and ferment at room temperature (68–72°F/20–22°C) overnight, 10–12 hours. The sponge will be very bubbly, have a clean sour smell, and will have tripled in volume.

Berlin One-Stage Quick Sponge (Hydration 100%)

When I'm rushed for time or have forgotten to start my sponge the night before bake day, the Berlin quick sponge[60] lets me have my rye bread and eat it too, so to speak. Used in conjunction with commercial yeast or a yeasted wheat sponge, this method gives me a beautifully balanced sour sponge in less than 4 hours—meaning that I can start almost any of my light and medium rye breads (which don't need to season for a day or two before slicing), in the morning and enjoy them that evening. The "Lifted" Country Boule (page 215) offers a great example of how nicely this technique works.

The secret lies in the relatively large amount of sour culture—20% versus the more usual 8–10%—in the sponge formula, the warmth of the water, and short, high-temperature ferment at 95°F/35°C—the sweet spot at which LAB activity peaks (see the graph on page 33), but at which yeast activity grinds to a virtual standstill. After about 3¼ hours, I have a robust acidifying sponge in which lactic acid predominates; if I let it go longer, the LAB start producing acetic acid, so that after 3¾ hours the sponge has developed a well-rounded yet unobtrusive acidity profile. Although the brevity of the Berlin method makes it impractical for commercial bakers, since it demands attention and heat during peak baking times, it's great for home bakers. Just remember the commercial yeast, on pain of ending up with a doorstop instead of an edible loaf.

INGREDIENT	GRAMS	OUNCES	BAKER'S PERCENTAGE
Medium rye flour	100	3.55	100%
Warm (105°F/41°C) water	100	3.55	100%
Rye sour culture	20	0.70	20%

Mix the sponge ingredients by hand until incorporated, cover, and ferment at 95°F/35°C in a warming oven or proofing cabinet for 3¼–3¾ hours. The sponge will be bubbly and have a clean sour smell. If a warming oven or proofing cabinet isn't available, preheat the oven to 100°F/38°C, then turn it off and place the sponge inside. Reheat to 100°F/38°C every hour until the sponge has fully ripened.

Basic Two-Stage Sponge

Two-stage sponges use a base sponge that's allowed to ripen into a Type II sponge and then given a second feeding of rye flour and water. The chief advantage of two-stage sponges is their long fermentation time and yeast-acid balance: commercial bakers love them because they can mix Stage 1 on Saturday night and mix Stage 2 on Monday morning with no appreciable loss of leavening power or acidity. A basic two-stage sponge achieves balance by favoring yeast activity and acetic acid production in the first stage and balancing out the acidity profile with lactic acidification in Stage 2.

STAGE 1: BASE SOUR (HYDRATION 50%; DAY 1, EVENING)

INGREDIENT	GRAMS	OUNCES	BAKER'S PERCENTAGE
Medium or whole-grain rye flour	50	1.75	100%
Warm (105°F/41°C) water	25	0.90	50%
Rye sour culture	5	0.20	10%

Ferment for 15–35 hours at 73–81°F/23–27°C.

STAGE 2: FULL SOUR (HYDRATION 80%; DAY 2, AFTERNOON/DAY 3, MORNING)

INGREDIENT	GRAMS	OUNCES	BAKER'S PERCENTAGE
Stage 1 sour	80	2.85	160%
Medium or whole-grain rye flour	50	1.75	100%
Water	55	2.00	110%

Ferment for 3 hours at 77–82°F/25–28°C.

Note that there can be lots of variations on two-stage sponges. In the recipes that follow, Stage 2 additions include not only rye flour and water in varying proportions but also sweeteners, spices, and salt. Their fermentation times and temperatures also can vary. I haven't found any logic to these diverse Stage 2 feedings, except, perhaps, to conclude that they reflect the customs and sensibilities of the regions in which the various breads originated.

Basic Three-Stage Sponge

For more robust, well-balanced Type I sponges, three-stage fermentation at varying hydration levels manages the activity of yeast and LAB separately. This basic three-stage sponge provides considerable latitude of sponge hydration, fermentation time, and temperature. When I want a more robust, more acidic sponge, this is the one I use.

STAGE 1: YEAST REFRESHMENT (HYDRATION 100–120%; DAY 1, MORNING)

INGREDIENT	GRAMS	OUNCES	BAKER'S PERCENTAGE
Medium or whole-grain rye flour	50	1.75	100%
Warm (105°F/41°C) water	50–60	1.75–2.15	100–120%
Rye sour culture	5	0.20	10%

The first stage is aimed primarily at increasing the yeast concentration. At 100–120% hydration, it's a relatively wet sponge that ripens for 5–8 hours at 77–80°F/25–26°C—the temperature range in which yeast activity peaks (see the graph on page 33).

STAGE 2: ACIDIFICATION SOUR (HYDRATION 50–60%; DAY 1, EVENING)

INGREDIENT	GRAMS	OUNCES	BAKER'S PERCENTAGE
Refreshment sour	105–115	3.70–4.05	210–230%
Medium or whole-grain rye flour	50	1.75	100%
Water	0–10	0–0.35	0–20%

The goal of Stage 2 is to increase the acetic acid level of the sponge; hence the drastic reduction of its total hydration to 50–70%, increased ripening time of 6–10 hours, and wider temperature range of 73–82°F/23–28°C.

STAGE 3: FULL SOUR (HYDRATION 78–88%; DAY 2, MORNING)

INGREDIENT	GRAMS	OUNCES	BAKER'S PERCENTAGE
Acidification sour	155–175	7.00–7.55	155–175%
Medium or whole-grain rye flour	100	3.55	100%
Warm (105°F/41°C) water	105–115	3.70–4.05	105–115%

Stage 3 is where full ripening takes place, balancing out both the yeast and the acidity. Hydration increases to 78–88% for the total sponge, and fermentation lasts for 3–10 hours at the still wider temperature range of 77–90°F/25–32°C, fostering optimal yeast and LAB activity.

Detmold Three-Stage Sponge

With the precision they're noted for, the scientists at the Max Rübner Institute–German Federal Research Institute for Nutrition and Food (*Max Rubner-Institut, Bundesforschungsinstitut für Ernährung und Lebensmittel*) (MRI) in Detmold, Germany, have refined the Basic Three-Stage Sponge to what I can only describe as high art that demands close attention to every aspect of its fermentation. Unlike the basic three-stage sponge, the Detmold sponge technique calls for exact temperatures and hydration levels. Done correctly, with a minimum of 40% total flour weight, Detmold is the ultimate sour sponge, contributing both intense, memorable flavor and a tender, open crumb to breads that don't need additional leavening.

STAGE 1: YEAST REFRESHMENT (HYDRATION 150%; DAY 1, MORNING)

INGREDIENT	GRAMS	OUNCES	BAKER'S PERCENTAGE
Medium or whole-grain rye flour	50	1.75	100%
Water	76	2.70	152%
Rye sour culture	5	0.20	10%

Ferment for 6 hours at 77–80°F/25–26°C.

STAGE 2: ACIDIFICATION (HYDRATION 63%; DAY 1, AFTERNOON)

INGREDIENT	GRAMS	OUNCES	BAKER'S PERCENTAGE
Refreshment sour	131	4.60	181%
Medium or whole-grain rye flour	71	2.50	100%
Water	0	0	0%

Ferment for 15–25 hours at 86°F/30°C.

INGREDIENT	GRAMS	OUNCES	BAKER'S PERCENTAGE
Acidification sour	202	7.15	202%
Medium or whole-grain rye flour	100	3.55	100%
Water	122	4.30	122%

Ferment 3 hours at 82°F/28°C.

Monheimer Salt Sponge

The Monheimer sponge, which adds about 2% salt to a standard single-stage sponge, was developed in the late 1950s as a way of shortening the ripening time of Type II acidifying sponges, which typically require 1–7 days. The chemistry works because salt is a yeast inhibitor that curtails its ability to compete with the LAB for the sugars produced by enzyme activity. The fast pace of the sponge's development comes from its high 20% rye starter culture component and 16-hour fermentation at a high initial temperature of 95°F/35°C, falling to 68°F/20°C. These factors produce an intensely sour acidifying sponge that requires the addition of commercial yeast in the final dough. Sauerland Black Bread (page 348) uses a Monheimer sponge to produce a well-balanced flavor profile of sour, sweet, and nutty.

INGREDIENT	GRAMS	OUNCES	BAKER'S PERCENTAGE
Medium or whole-grain rye flour	100	3.55	100%
Warm (105°F/41°C) water	100	3.55	100%
Salt	2	0.10	2%
Rye sour culture	20	0.65	20%

Nonfermented Predoughs

Nonfermented predoughs are simply doughs to which no leavening or fermenting agent has been added. In rye baking, and especially in whole-grain and rustic breads, they take two forms— soakers and scalds. Both serve the function of softening dry ingredients and bringing their nutrients into solution, where they become available to the microorganisms and enzymes that populate both the predough and final dough. As a result both soakers and scalds enhance the tenderness of the crumb and add new dimensions of flavor to breads that use them.

Soakers

A soaker is a nutrient-rich mix that boosts LAB and yeast activity in the dough and adds deeper layers of flavor to the finished breads. A typical soaker consists of cool (60–85°F/15–30°C) water and dry ingredients totaling 30–50% of total flour weight left to stand at room temperature (68–72°F/20–22°C) for 10–20 hours.

Functionally, softening and hydrating dry ingredients like rye meal and cracked wheat, nuts, and seeds, dried fruit, and stale bread before they're incorporated into the dough releases their sugars, starches, and oils into solution. These nutrients then become available to the LAB, yeast, and amylase enzymes present in the grain's outer layers and kick-start fermentation when the soaker is added to the final dough. Importantly, presoaking also prevents the dry ingredients from attracting water away from the dough, which would produce hard, dry loaves that have an unpleasantly gritty mouthfeel.

Soakers are used widely in rye baking, especially in breads containing large amounts of seeds, nuts, and/or coarsely milled grain, such as Pumpkinseed Rye (page 131), Rhineland Black Bread (page 314), Valais Rye (page 235), and Hearty Seeded Rye (page 157).

Scalds

Scalds are soakers that combine whole-grain flours and coarsely milled grains with hot (150–175°F/65–80°C) or boiling water. A typical scald contains 20–40% of a recipe's total flour at 80–150% hydration and stands for 2–24 hours at room temperature (68–72°F/20–22°C). Scalds add sweetness, tenderness, and moisture to rye breads, softening their crumb and improving their holding quality.

The chemistry of scalds causes me to stand in awe of the generations of ordinary bakers who devised them. The hot water effectively kills off the yeast and LAB, which can't survive temperatures above 140°F/60°C. At the same time, it creates the ideal environment for amylase activity, which peaks at 140–170°F/60–77°C. As a result, scalds not only soften and hydrate coarse grains but also create high concentrations of natural sugars that provide a power boost to yeast and LAB activity in the final dough and add sweetness to the finished breads. Scalds play a key role in slow-baked and coarse high-percentage rye breads like Slow-Baked Frisian Rye (page 155), Danish Rye Bread (page 127), Sweet-Sour Rye Bread (page 250) and Westphalian Pumpernickel (page 336).

Compound Sponges

During my journey into the world of rye, I discovered a class of predoughs that I never imagined existed—compound preferments that marry a scald to a sponge before the final dough is mixed. I've encountered these scald-sponges, as I call them, only in Russian and Baltic ryes—intensely sour breads whose flavor profiles are rich with subtle sweetness and the astringency of caraway and coriander.

In each instance the scald brings high concentrations of natural sugars to robust sour sponges that have typically ripened overnight. The combined scald-sponges ripen at room temperature (68–72°F/20–22°C) for anywhere from 2 to 18 hours, producing an extraordinarily clean sour, underlain with the burnt caramel sweetness of the sugar-rich rye scald.

For the most part, scald-sponges account for one stage in a multistage recipe, as in the GOST Borodinsky (page 253) and Latvian Sweet-Sour Rye Bread (page 250). There is, however, one bread—Belarusian Sweet Rye (page 277)—that I regard as the ultimate expression of the rye baker's art. Instead of one or two stages, Sweet Rye is progressively built on a sour sponge, a malted rye scald, a rye scald-sour, a potato scald, and a yeasted potato-rye scald-sour that Russian bakers call an *opara*—all before the final dough is mixed. Yes, the bread is complex and time consuming, but to me every second is worth it for the layer upon layer of flavor—sweet, malty, sour, chocolate, coffee—that lie hidden in the ingredients, just waiting for the baker's hand to coax them forth.

3. MIXING

The final dough brings together all of a bread's components—predoughs, if any, and a range of ingredients that typically includes flour, hydrating liquid (water, milk, beer), salt, yeast, fats, sweeteners, flavoring agents, proteins and/or vegetables, and textural components like seeds, nuts, and coarsely milled grains. The act of mixing not only distributes ingredients evenly throughout the dough but also sets off a round of physical and chemical activity that unlocks and integrates the flavors, textures, microbes, enzymes, and their by-products present in the predoughs, if any, with the storehouse of unreleased flavors, textures, and chemistry locked inside the raw ingredients.

Mixing at low speed works best. For the sake of consistency, I use KitchenAid settings to indicate mixing speeds, so that lowest speed is written as KA1, low as KA2, and low-medium as KA4. No matter what kind of bread I'm making, I aim for a final dough temperature in the range of 72–82°F/22–28°C.

Rye doughs can exhibit a variety of textures and behaviors, depending on their composition and hydration. Light rye breads containing 50% or more wheat flour, for example, need longer mixing and kneading to initiate the gluten formation that provides structure to the loaf. For those doughs I generally use the dough hook and mix at low (KA2) speed until the dough is fully developed and leaves the sides of the mixing bowl. Of note, a few higher-percentage rye doughs, like Minsk Rye (page 267), Scorched-Crust Sour Rye (page 137), and Breton Folded Rye (page 105), which have hydration levels in the low-to-mid-60% range, also clean the bowl and gather around the dough hook during mixing, but they're the exception.

Medium- and high-percentage ryes—those with more than 50% rye—have lesser amounts of gluten to develop, so all that's needed is to mix until the dough comes together as an integrated, evenly blended mass—which can take less or more time, depending on the hydration level and flour texture.

The paddle works best for mixing dense, coarse-textured doughs, for example, Westphalian Pumpernickel (page 336), Ammerland Black Bread (page 151), and Hearty Seeded Rye (page 157), precisely because they don't form gluten. Instead of pulling away from the sides of the bowl and gathering around the dough hook like a well-behaved wheat dough, coarse high-percentage rye doughs do just the opposite—they cling tenaciously to the bowl wall, thumbing their figurative noses as the dough hook spins around in vain, barely grazing their surface. And even though the paddle has less clearance from the sides of the bowl and so does a better job of bringing the dough together, I find that I still have to stand around, spatula in hand, to pry those refractory doughs back into the path of the spinning paddle.

One technique I've developed to minimize all that bowl scraping is to build my sponges in the mixer bowl itself, which also reduces waste and cuts down on bowl washing, then add the dry ingredients, liquids, soakers and/or scalds, if any, in that order. By sandwiching the dry ingredients between wet layers, I avoid the pang I invariably feel when I empty a bowl of what I think is a well-integrated dough, only to find a big pocket of unmixed flour at the bottom. Even if I build my sponge in a separate container, it's first into the mixer.

4. BULK FERMENTATION

In both wheat and rye doughs, the bulk fermentation stage is where most of the chemistry happens. Enzymes metabolize starches into sugars that yeast and LAB feed on, while molecules of salt, protein, fats, esters, and the whole panoply of other substances that together shape a bread's character and personality engage in their magical dance.

When I first started working with rye, the books I read—all of them focused on wheat breads, with a nod or two in rye's direction—warned about the speed of rye fermentation, the instability of the dough, and the need for vigilance so as not to miss its narrow window of peak development. As my experience grew, however, I learned that rye doughs, especially those with a large sour sponge component, are really pretty time tolerant, with average bulk fermentation times of 1 hour or longer—a few fermenting for as long as 5 or 6 hours.

The important variables in bulk fermentation are dough temperature after mixing and ambient temperature. In general, warmer means faster, but often at the cost of less acidity, since yeast acts more quickly than LAB. In my own baking I aim for a final dough temperature in the range of 72–82°F/22–28°C and ferment most of my doughs at my kitchen temperature, which averages 70°F/21°C in winter and 78°F/25°C in summer. To keep things simple, I ferment my doughs in the mixer bowl, since they don't need folding or other postmix handling—with the one exception of Auvergne Rye-Wheat Boule (page 111). It also simplifies clean-up.

Judging when to bring the fermentation stage to an end is more a matter of feel and experience than of clock watching; it's my eyes, nose, and fingers that really tell me what's happening with my dough. A lot of it, of course, is knowing what to look for: smooth-textured doughs are ready for benching (see below) when they've expanded to 1½–2 times their original volume, depending on texture, and have a clean sour smell. Coarse doughs, on the other hand, may show little or no expansion but ask that I rely on the clock and my nose to judge their maturity. Because no two kitchens, bakeries, or doughs are identical, I give ranges of fermentation and proofing times, but these are intended only as a guide for checking the dough's progress.

5. BENCHING

I use the term *benching* to include everything I do to a dough between fermentation and proofing, which typically includes degassing, dividing, shaping, and panning.

This is probably a good place to talk about rye's legendary stickiness, which stems from the immutable fact of life that a viscous gel composed of complex carbohydrates (arabinoxylans; see page 31) and water is what holds rye doughs together. Working with rye is all about learning to love, or at least tolerate, sticky: rye doughs, especially wet ones, cling tenaciously to everything they touch and, unless wiped up immediately, dry to concrete hardness. This sticky reality informs every aspect of benching rye.

Two substances, flour and water, keep rye doughs manageable during benching, and both work equally well, although wetting a work surface can get both messy and slimy. I use water to keep my scrapers, bench knives, and spatulas cling free when I move dough from the mixer and flour for my work surface, scraper, and hands while I handle the dough.

The logic behind degassing is that it reduces the amount of CO_2, a yeast inhibitor produced during bulk fermentation and paves the way for vigorous proofing. Because rye dough is such a nutrient-rich environment, I degas my doughs as much as possible by hand-kneading them back to their original volume. Some doughs, however, never touch a work surface but go directly into a pan; they're the heavily yeasted (either commercial or sponge) breads like Slow-Baked Finnish Rye (page 190) and Breton Folded Rye Bread (page 105), or they're unleavened steamed breads like Slow-Baked Frisian Rye (page 155) and Westphalian Pupernickel (page 336).

Division is pretty straightforward. With the help of my trusty bench knife (dough scraper) and digital scale, I simply cut the dough into as many pieces as the recipe calls for, weighing each to keep the size consistent. To prevent dough from sticking to my scale, I make sure to weigh it floured side down.

Unlike wheat doughs, medium- and high-percentage rye doughs don't require either preshaping or resting, nor, in fact do light ryes, since the rye flour seems to bring its own brand of relaxation to the gluten. Shaping, therefore, is also straightforward. The only imperative I've found in shaping is to strive for a smooth surface and a single seam, no matter what the dough's rye content or whether the loaf is a ball (*boule*), oblong (*bâtard*), panned or bound for a proofing basket.

Whether a loaf is free-form or panned is as much a matter of custom and aesthetics as it is of dough consistency. Minsk Rye (page 267), Sweet Limpa (page 185), and Scorched-Crust Sour Rye (page 137) all have stiff doughs, but only the Minsk and Limpa are free-formed. Other breads, like Danish Rye Bread (page 127), Slow-Baked Finnish Rye (page 190), and Westphalian Pumpernickel (page 336), have doughs that are so dense or so coarse that only a pan will hold them. And still other breads, like the Austrian Country Boule (page 227) and Münster Country Boule (page 325), are customarily free-formed but have relatively slack doughs that require a basket for proper proofing.

6. PROOFING

Proofing is the final stage of yeast fermentation, where its production of CO_2 pushes the shaped loaf toward its limit of expansion. While proofing ideally should take place at temperatures in the range of 85–105°F/30–40°C, I've found that proofing my loaves at room temperature (68–72°F/20–22°C) takes a bit longer but produces equally good results.

On average, rye breads proof for about 45 minutes, but as with bulk fermentation, proofing times can vary considerably, depending on the composition of the dough and the bulk fermentation time. Ammerland Black Bread (page 151), for example, proofs for 2½–3 hours, but that's because it goes directly from mixer to pan, with no bulk fermentation. Zakopane Buttermilk Rye (page 299), on the other hand, proofs for 1–1½ hours after fermenting for just 20–30 minutes. And Galician Rye Bread (page 107), which ferments for 2–2½ hours, proofs for less than 10 minutes.

Note that the proofing times for each recipe are only approximations, again, because each kitchen and each batch of dough is different, even if only in subtle ways. Over the years I've learned that my eyes and nose tell me best that my loaves are ready for the oven. In the case of panned breads I look for the dough to have risen within ½ inch/1.25 cm of the rim and also the first sign of cracking or broken bubbles on the surface of the dough. For unpanned breads I look for both expansion and cracks or bubbles; when they appear, it's bake time.

One caveat: keep a close eye on the dough as it approaches the late stages of its proof. Unlike bulk fermentation, which has a fairly broad window, rye breads—especially high-percentage loaves—can overproof quickly, resulting in an unpleasantly dense, gummy loaf. Conversely, underproofing can also be a problem: there have been times, I regret to say, that I put my loaf in too early, only to earn myself an oven floor encrusted with charred overflow or, in one really bad case, a bread that literally exploded, leaving shards of dough adhering to every surface of my beautiful high-tech oven. Not only were the breads disappointing, but the cleanup was pure drudgery. To quote Arthur Miller in *Death of a Salesman*, "Attention must be paid."

7. PREBAKE

The few minutes before a loaf goes into the oven is the last time I can influence its taste, behavior during baking, and most aspects of its appearance. One problem I've encountered a lot working with rye is a blown loaf, which happens when a crust ruptures because the steam generated during baking can't find another way out. Deliberately creating weakness in the crust directs its oven spring and reduces the likelihood of blown loaves. I can slash it, which springs the loaf along the cuts, or I can dock it—that is, prick the crust with a fork, chopstick, skewer, or docking wheel (which looks like a spike-studded paint roller). To ensure proper expansion, or nonexpansion, of the bread I make sure to slash or dock the crust to a depth of at least ¼–½ inch/0.6–1.25 cm.

Prebake is also the time to brush or mist the top crust with water so that it doesn't set too quickly, add seeds or other toppings, or apply the flour-water slurry that gives the Cumin Rye (page 290) and other breads their shiny crust.

8. BAKING

The application of high heat brings one set of chemical and physical changes to an end and initiates another in the metamorphosis of flour and water into a finished loaf of bread.

Rye baking steps down oven temperature in a way wheat baking generally doesn't, which I believe mimics the behavior of wood-fired ovens, whose thick walls retained the heat that baked our bread for most of human history. Although I neither own nor have access to a wood-fired oven, I can approximate its behavior in my home oven by means of a baking stone (or two). Stones are available in a variety of ceramic materials and even steel; mine is a ⅝-inch/1.5 cm thick slab of cordierite, a high-performance ceramic large enough to fit my oven with a margin of 1 inch/2.5 cm on each side for heat circulation. I also keep a second stone above the baking surface to radiate heat downward, again re-creating as much as possible the 360-degree radiant heat environment in a wood-fired oven.

A baking stone performs two functions that standard oven racks can't: First, it provides a blazing-hot surface on which I can bake my free-form loaves directly, producing a thick and crispy bottom crust that's unattainable on a sheet pan. Second—and perhaps more important—it absorbs and holds heat, which reduces or eliminates the hot spots found in almost all home ovens, providing even heat throughout my bake and freeing me from having to turn my loaves halfway through to get even browning.

With a few exceptions—mainly in the quick breads, rolls, and American rye breads—most European rye breads start their bake in the range of 450–500°F/230–260°C. This high temperature causes the water carried near the dough's surface to literally explode into steam, maximizing oven spring. After 5 or 10 minutes, once the loaf has reached its maximum spring, the oven temperature moderates downward to a range of 350–425°F/175–220°C, where baking finishes.

Rye baking also uses a lot of steam, which conducts heat more efficiently than air and also keeps the crust moist and flexible while the loaf springs. When I want steam, I preheat my oven with the otherwise useless enameled broiler pan that came with it on a shelf below the baking stone. Five minutes before bake time,

I pour 227–340 ml/8–12 oz./1–1½ cups of boiling water, depending on how long the breads will steam, into the pan, wearing a silicone mitt to avoid steam burns. After steaming I remove the pan and keep the oven door open for 20–30 seconds or so to let the rest of the steam escape and lower the oven temperature, then reset the thermostat and finish my bake.

The heat of baking initiates changes in a fixed order. During the early stages yeast metabolism skyrockets, generating large amounts of CO_2 that get trapped in the dough and create the oven spring that swells the loaf toward its final dimensions. As the heat penetrates, raising the internal temperature above 140°F/60°C, the yeast and LAB die off, leaving an open field for the amylase enzymes to step up their starch attack.

Amylase activity, which peaks at 140–160°F/60–71°C and ceases entirely at 176°F/80°C, poses a particular challenge for high-percentage rye breads. In the absence of a gluten lattice to support the loaf, high-percentage ryes depend on the starchy arabinoxylan gels for their structure. Unchecked, amylase activity degrades the arabinoxylans into sugars that can't support the bread, resulting in collapsed, gummy loaves. As noted earlier, however (see page 32), moderately to highly acid environments (pH 5.0–3.2) impede amylase activity, allowing the arabinoxylans to harden so that the breads develop an open crumb and firm structure—which is why most high-percentage ryes start with sour sponges that preferment anywhere from 30% to 60% of the total flour in the recipe.

One class of breads. the slow bakes, embrace amylase activity instead of trying to avoid it. These breads—Slow-Baked Finnish Rye (page 190), Slow-Baked Frisian Rye (page 155), Boston Brown Bread (page 91), and Westphalian Pumpernickel (page 336)—all cook low and slow, in sealed pans, at temperatures of 200–230°F/95–110°C for anywhere from 3 to 24 hours. In fact, these slow bakes are less breads in the conventional sense than they are steamed puddings. Whatever they are, they're special: the slowly rising internal temperature creates ideal conditions for the amylase enzymes to transform starches into sugars, while the prolonged heat creates a deeply caramelized crumb, producing dense, almost black breads whose dominant sweetness carries dark, slightly burnt molasses notes.

Heat also influences a bread's structure. At 140°F/60°C the hydrated starches start to gelatinize, and at 145°F/63°C gluten starts to harden. At 160°F/71°C the gluten structure is fully coagulated, and at 194°F/90°C the gelatinization of the starches is complete.

Only the browning of the crust remains, but that's a crucial step. By the time the loaf's crust temperature reaches 212°F/100°C, all of the surface moisture has evaporated and rapid warming begins. At about 230°F/115°C, the Maillard reaction—which refers to the caramelization of the crust, browning proteins, sugars, and gelatinized starches—kicks in. As the surface temperature approaches 350°F/177°C, the

Maillard reaction ceases and crust browning is complete. During this stage the heat also causes ingredients in the crust area to break down into aldehydes and ketones, volatile elements that contribute to a loaf's flavor and produce the ineffable aroma of baking bread, which tells my nose when the baking's done.

Occasionally a recipe calls for an interruption of baking. Two of the breads, GOST Borodinsky (page 253) and Scorched-Crust Sour Rye (page 137), bake in two stages, first in the pan, then unpanned and returned to the oven to crisp the side and bottom crusts. Glazing a bread's crust to a lustrous sheen also entails interrupting the bake to brush or spray the loaves with water, as for Kassel Rye (page 333) and Cumin Rye (page 290), or beer in the case of Caraway Beer Bread (page 231).

9. POSTBAKE AND STORAGE

Baking doesn't stop when the bread comes out of the oven but continues until it reaches room temperature. Gases continue to escape, resulting in collapsed centers in loaves that don't have a structure strong enough to support the crumb. Starches and proteins bond and solidify, firming the crumb, and moisture moves outward, softening the crust. Many of the volatile aromatic compounds dissipate, causing the aroma of warm bread to fade, while the remaining aromatic and flavor components disperse through crumb and crust.

There are a couple of steps to take as soon as the bread comes out of the oven. The first is brushing a cornstarch glaze on the Old-School Deli Rye (page 80), New York Corn Rye (page 87), and Jewish Bakery Pumpernickel (page 93). This glaze both tenderizes the crust and slows the escape of baking gases, keeping the breads especially moist for a day or two. It's important, though, to do it while the breads are still near oven temperature, since applying the glaze to breads that have cooled slightly makes for a hazy crust.

The second postbake step to be taken immediately is moistening the crusts with boiling water, especially of high-percentage ryes baked at high temperature, so as to keep the crumb moist while the loaf seasons.

Unlike wheat breads, which stale quickly, rye breads are built to last. The high water absorbency of the arabinoxylan starches and the resistance of sourdoughs to the toughening—called *retrogradation*—of gelatinized starches that causes wheat breads to go stale in a few days can keep rye breads moist and fresh for a week to 10 days. Resting the loaves for a day or two after they come out of the oven also improves flavor. In fact, the longer I let my high-percentage rye breads stand uncut, the better they taste. After they've cooled to room temperature, I generally wrap them in plastic and let them rest for two to four days. While resting, the crust softens, the starches in the crumb stabilize and lose their gumminess, and the flavor elements released during baking disperse evenly through the bread. A bread that's gummy and bitter 3 hours after it comes out of the oven develops an even crumb and clean flavor profile 3 or 4 days later.

And on those rare occasions when I have more rye bread than my family, my friends, and I can eat in a week, it goes into the freezer, where it keeps beautifully. I just need to keep the loaves tightly wrapped in plastic to minimize moisture loss. To defrost, I leave them out at room temperature overnight. And that's really all there is to it.

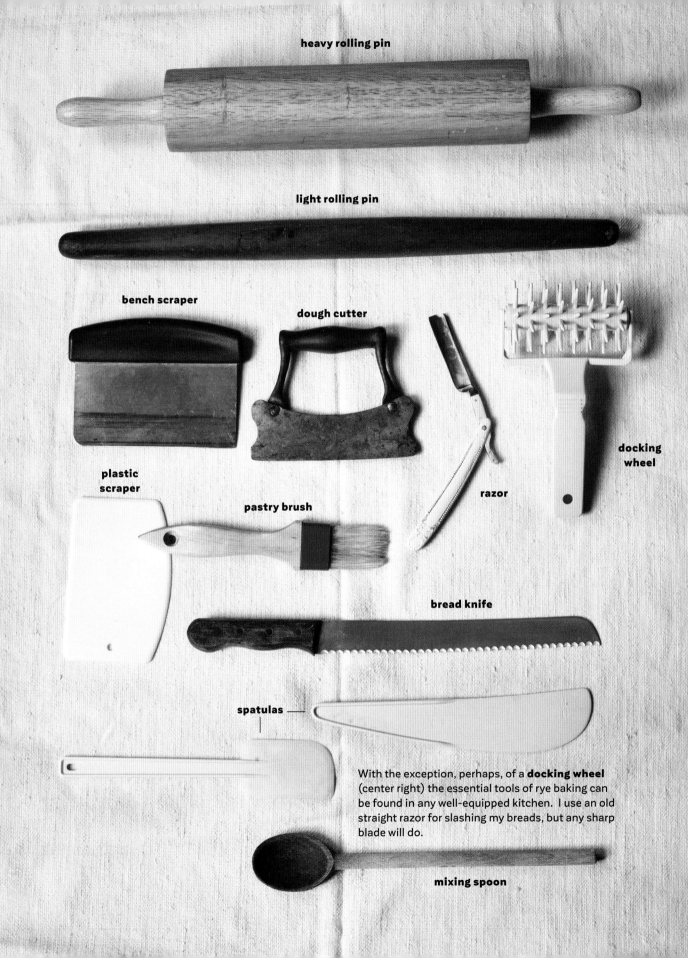

heavy rolling pin

light rolling pin

bench scraper

dough cutter

docking wheel

plastic scraper

pastry brush

razor

bread knife

spatulas

With the exception, perhaps, of a **docking wheel** (center right) the essential tools of rye baking can be found in any well-equipped kitchen. I use an old straight razor for slashing my breads, but any sharp blade will do.

mixing spoon

Equipment

Lots of utensils and supplies come into play in baking rye. Fortunately, most of them are already part of a well-equipped kitchen, and those that aren't are easy to come by. For simplicity's sake, I present them according to how they're used.

INGREDIENT PREPARATION

For slicing, dicing, and mincing, nothing beats a **chef's knife and cutting board**, preferably polyethylene. For shredding vegetables, I use a **mandoline**. Although many cookbooks recommend food processors to chop nuts, I find that it's too easy to overprocess; instead, I use an old-fashioned **wooden bowl and semicircular chopping knife**, which not only produce a better result but require much less cleanup.

For grating, I use a **Microplane zester** for things like nutmeg and citrus zest and an old-fashioned **box grater** for cheese and raw vegetables.

The amount of grinding I need to do determines which tool I use. For small quantities of spices and malted grain, I use an **electric spice grinder**. When I have to grind larger quantities—say, if I've roasted a pound of malted rye and want to turn it into flour, or if I need something I can't find commercially, such as cracked spelt—I use the **grain-milling accessory** for my stand mixer. That, however, is a luxury that I like having but suspect most people won't need.

Some recipes call for heating ingredients before baking takes place—for example, warming, sautéing, and toasting rye malt, seeds, or spices. For this, use an **ordinary skillet or saucepan**; for oven-toasting larger quantities, spread them on a **sheet pan**.

MEASUREMENT

Scale

Next to an oven, an accurate scale is indispensable for consistent results. Volume measurements can vary widely. The weight of 1 cup of flour, for example, will be different in dry versus humid climates or for flour that's densely packed versus sifted; 500 grams of flour, on the other hand, always weighs 500 grams.

There are any number of good, inexpensive digital scales on the market. As a home baker, the scale I've found most useful has a capacity of at least 11 lb./5 kg—enough to accommodate large batches of dough, plus mixing bowl—and reads out in increments of 1 gram and 0.05 oz. The tare feature, which resets the readout of a loaded scale to zero, is an extremely useful standard feature on all digital scales. By zeroing my scale after each addition, I can measure directly into the mixing bowl without having to weigh each ingredient separately.

Because digital scales can read out in negative numbers, the tare function is also useful for weighing ingredients that otherwise can be challenging. Sour culture, for example, sticks tenaciously to everything it touches, making it difficult to add the right amount of culture to a sponge. By zeroing the scale with the sour culture container on it and removing the culture with my mixing spoon, I get a negative readout that tells me exactly how much sour culture is going into my sponge.

Measuring Cups and Spoons

For people who prefer to measure by volume, measuring cups and spoons are a necessity. Since I weigh everything, I don't use either; instead, I let the scale do the work. For small quantities, I use regular teaspoons and tablespoons and, for larger quantities, a flour scoop for dry ingredients, a measuring cup (because of the lip and handle) for water, and pour other liquid ingredients directly from the container.

Thermometers

I use two handheld thermometers to measure ingredient temperatures. My probe-type **instant-read digital thermometer** has a range of –40° to 450°F/–40° to 232°C and lets me measure internal temperatures during mixing and baking with a high degree of accuracy. For stovetop applications, such as boiling syrups and warming liquids, I use either the handheld probe or a dial-type **candy thermometer** that reads out from 50°F to 550°F/10°C to 287°C and clips onto the lip of a saucepan.

MIXING AND FERMENTATION

Electric mixers are the workhorses of baking, and there are many types on the market—spiral mixers, food processors, and tilt-head and fixed-head stand mixers for example. I use a fixed-head 6-quart stand mixer equipped with a paddle for heavy mixing and dough hook for developing doughs. I like it because it's easy to keep clean, big enough to handle all of the recipes in this book, and small enough to fit in a cabinet under my counter.

More than other breads, ryes use lots of **bowls and covered plastic containers**—for sour culture, sponges, soakers, scalds, compound predoughs, fillings, and the doughs themselves. I use a small stainless-steel bowl to refresh my sour culture, which I immediately transfer to a covered plastic container for ripening and storage. I use both the plastic containers and porcelain, glass, and stainless-steel bowls, covered with either plastic wrap or a dinner plate, for my predoughs, and I use

the mixer bowl for both mixing and bulk fermenting final doughs. If I need the mixer for another batch, I transfer the dough to a large **stainless-steel, glass, or stoneware bowl** for fermentation.

Spoons and whisks are the original mixers. I use both wooden and metal spoons to hand-mix sponges, scalds, soakers, and highly hydrated doughs. Whisks are useful for blending dry ingredients or for dissolving sponges, yeast, and syrups in water or milk.

A variety of plastic and metal **scrapers and spatulas** is indispensable for moving sticky rye doughs from one place to another. To transfer sponges, soakers, and scalds to the mixer and to scrape down the bowl during mixing, I use a **silicone- or nylon-bladed spatula**.

To cover the bowl in which my dough ferments, I use a **dinner plate or pot lid**, which both prevents drying and eliminates the need for plastic wrap.

BENCHING

Any smooth, hard **work surface**—wood, marble, granite, synthetic stone, stainless steel, polyethylene, or laminate—will do; just be sure to have enough room to work

comfortably. Clean it by hand, using a scraper to loosen dried dough and gather loose flour, then wiping it down with a damp cloth or paper towel. If you're thinking about buying something, I recommend a wooden cutting board at least 22 inches/55 cm wide and 18 inches/45 cm deep. Give it a generous coating of USP mineral oil (vegetable oils can turn rancid) before first use and every few months thereafter.

For moving the developed dough from mixer to work surface, I use a **plastic dough scraper** with one square and one rounded edge; and for working, shaping, and dividing the dough, a 6-by-4-inch/15-by-10 cm **metal-bladed dough scraper** is my implement of choice. A **scale** is also useful for ensuring that my loaves and rolls are sized equally.

For cutting crsipbreads in the pan I use a **pizza wheel**, and for punching out the center of circular loaves a **round cookie cutter**, although a **shot glass** or **juice glass** will work just as well.

PROOFING

If you're using a baking stone, proof your free-form loaves directly on a well-floured **wooden proofing board** or **bakers' peel**. For rolls and when you don't have a baking stone, use a **sheet pan** lined with **parchment paper**.

For slack doughs, use a well-floured **proofing basket**—either a linen-lined French *banneton* or a German *brotform* made of coiled rattan. The baskets not only support the dough during proofing but also, because of the absorbency of their materials, wick moisture away from the surface of the dough, leaving a thin skin that makes for a thin, crisp crust. Before I acquired my proofing baskets I used **plastic bread baskets lined with linen napkins** after I learned the hard way that dough clings tenaciously to cotton but comes away cleanly from linen.

For panned breads the size and shape of the pan make a difference. When I started baking rye, I used my 9-by-5-by-3-inch/23-by-13-by-8 cm and 8½-by-4½-by-2¾-inch/22-by-12-by-7 cm **standard loaf pans**, well greased with vegetable shortening. I soon found, however, that rye doesn't have nearly the oven spring of the wheat doughs I was used to, nor does the crust support a spring that goes higher than the rim. Even though my loaves tasted good, they came out of the oven flat and wide, reminding me of bricks.

After looking at photos of a lot of Central European loaves, I switched to **Pullman loaf pans** with a 4-by-4-inch/10-by-10 cm cross section in both 9-inch/23 cm and 13-inch/33 cm lengths, for most of my German and Northern breads. The higher sides give me loaves that have a square cross section and, I believe, allow for more even baking and a more uniform crumb. Some Russian breads, like the Raisin-Orange Rye (page 273), customarily are baked in round pans; for them, I use an 8-by-3-inch/20-by-8 cm round cake pan or 9-inch/23 cm **charlotte** mold.

A word on pan materials: I prefer **dark-colored steel** with a nonstick coating for

linen-lined *banneton*

rattan bread forms

rattan bread form

Pullman loaf pans

conventional loaf pans

To hold loose doughs while proofing, rye bakers use linen-lined **willow bannetons** and **coiled rattan bread forms** (*brotformen*). For baking, **standard loaf pans** (bottom) will do, but the square cross-section of Pullman pans produces a more even bake and a taller loaf.

loaf pans, and aluminum for sheet pans. Steel doesn't conduct heat as quickly as aluminum, so that a rye dough—which typically is denser than a wheat dough—can bake longer, allowing enough time for the center to finish cooking without developing a thick, overcooked crust. Aluminum works better for sheet pans because its high conductivity concentrates heat at the bottom of the dough, whether it be free-form loaves or rolls—mimicking the effects of a baking stone.

I don't use glass or ceramic pans because they retain heat far longer than either aluminum or steel and can overcook a loaf if it's not immediately unpanned. Nor do I use pans made of silicone, which neither conducts nor retains heat efficiently, resulting in unevenly baked breads with pale, soft crusts.

Most of the pan-proofed breads in this book use vegetable shortening as a release agent. A couple, however—Frisian Gingerbread (page 148) and Westphalian Pumpernickel (page 336) proof and bake in parchment-lined loaf pans.

How to line a pan with parchment

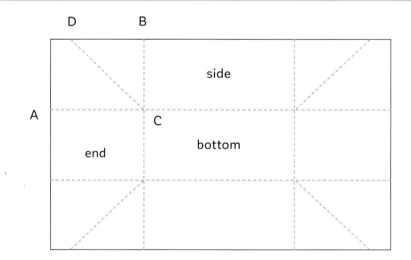

1. Place the pan in the center of a sheet of parchment and, using the base of the pan as a guide, use a dull pointed object like a table knife to score the parchment to about the dimensions of the inside bottom of the pan. Use a straightedge, such as a sheet pan, to extend the scoring to the edge of the parchment.

2. Fold the parchment along all four score lines and then unfold.

3. Bring folds A-C and B-C together and crease the parchment along diagonal D-C. Repeat for the other corners.

4. Place the parchment into the pan, bring the diagonal folds behind the ends, and secure them with a paper clip.

5. After filling the pan, remove the paper clips and either fold the parchment over the rim of the pan or trim it back to rim level.

To minimize drying, especially during a long proof, I cover my loaves with a damp **tea towel**, or, if the dough is especially sticky, lightly oiled **plastic wrap,** secured with a rubber band just below the lip of the pan.

PREBAKE

White bristle or silicone **pastry brushes**, which come in a variety of widths, are the easiest way to apply washes and glazes to breads and rolls both before and after baking. I prefer bristle over silicone because it holds more liquid and the softer bristles won't dent my dough. For misting a loaf before, during, and after the bake, nothing beats an ordinary **plastic spray bottle**.

To slash the dough before it goes into the oven any sharp blade will do; just be sure to cut deep enough, at least ¼–½ inch/0.6–1.25 cm. I use an old straight razor or a homemade *lâme* **(bread blade)**, which is nothing more than a double-edged razor blade that I bend into a C and slip onto a thin dowel or tapered chopstick.

For docking—that is, piercing the top crust multiple times to prevent rupture—I use a docking wheel, which looks like a cross between a paint roller and a porcupine. If you don't want to invest in one of those, use a **fork**, **chopstick**, or **bamboo skewer.** Dock the crust to a depth of at least ½ inch/1.25 cm.

BAKING

This may be obvious, but the **oven** is the single most important piece of equipment a baker can have. And since buying an oven isn't something we do every day, it's far more important to understand the oven you already have.

The reality is that no oven—not even the giant professional models that are larger than the typical New York apartment kitchen—heats evenly. Convection ovens solve the problem of uneven heat by using a fan or fans to move the hot air around inside the oven chamber. For this reason convection ovens cook more efficiently than standard ovens: a good rule of thumb for convection ovens is to reduce the baking temperature specified in this book by 25°F/15°C and cut baking times by 15–20%. Even better, use an instant-read probe thermometer to check loaf temperature.

Although convection ovens largely remedy uneven heating, the only way to check the accuracy of your oven's thermostat is with a couple of good-quality **oven thermometers**. Put them in different parts of the oven, recording the readings after 20–30 minutes, then switching them and noting any differences after another 20–30 minutes. With that information you can compare the average temperature of your oven with your thermostat setting. If you don't have a convection oven, move your thermometers around several more times so you can create an accurate heat map of your oven.

Although it certainly isn't necessary to go through this exercise to bake outstanding breads, the more you know about this key piece of equipment, the more control you'll have over your outcome.

Baking stones not only provide a nonstick, professional-quality surface but also absorb and hold heat. This property—called *thermal mass*—not only equalizes temperatures inside the oven but also reduces heat loss when the door is opened.

Baking stones come in many different shapes, sizes, and price ranges, from inexpensive ceramic "pizza stones" and materials like granite, soapstone, and unglazed quarry tiles to professional-grade refractory materials.

Which is better? The "pizza stones" produce the same crisp bottom crust as the professional ones but are notorious for cracking and losing heat. Natural stones also work well but may contain internal fractures or air bubbles that can cause them to come apart. Quarry tiles, depending on their origin and manufacture, may contain toxic substances that can leach into loaves.

The professional-grade stones are heavy, bulky, and take a long time to heat up; however, their compliance with food safety standards, greater thermal mass, and higher resistance to thermal shock—what happens when ice water meets a stone heated to 500°F/260°C—make them a much better choice.

If you do get a baking stone, be sure to get one that's at least ½–⅝ inch/ 1.25–1.5 cm thick and is the right size for your oven. A good rule of thumb for sizing is to leave 1 inch/2.5 cm of clearance on all sides to facilitate heat circulation; in other words, your stone should be 2 inches/5 cm shorter than the internal dimensions of your oven chamber.

Steam is one of the secrets to baking great rye breads. Creating a moist environment in the oven keeps the dough flexible longer than in a dry oven, allowing for greater expansion and a lighter, more open crumb. At the same time, the steam gelatinizes the bread's surface starches, producing a thin, glossy, and crisp crust. Since few home ovens come with steam injectors, all the home bakers I know use a **steam pan**.

There are as many opinions about optimal steaming as there are home bakers. Some swear by cast-iron pans, while others prefer aluminum or high-temperature ceramic—placed either above or below the bread. Some add lava rocks or a pound of 10-penny nails to the pan to increase surface area, which speeds up steam production. The water may be hot, cold, or even ice cubes. The debate goes on.

In my view all of those approaches are valid, except for the ice cubes, which require about 5,000 more heat-stealing BTUs per 1 oz./28.35 g than boiling water to turn into steam. That said, when I want steam, I preheat my oven with the otherwise useless enameled broiler pan that came with it on a shelf below the baking stone and add a cup or two of boiling water 5 minutes before bake time.

POSTBAKE AND STORAGE

The most efficient cooling occurs when air can circulate freely around all sides of the finished bread. For loaves I use a **wire cooling rack**, making sure to unpan the breads immediately. For rolls I use **open-weave willow or wicker baskets**, which both allow the air to circulate freely and take up far less counter space than a rack big enough to hold a couple dozen rolls.

After they've cooled, I keep my breads in regular **plastic bags**—especially if I want the crust to soften—or in **microperforated bakery bags**, which allow the air to circulate, minimizing the possibility of mold.

Immigrant Bread: America

THE story of American rye breads is the story in microcosm of America itself.

Like the immigrants who brought them, those strong-flavored black breads came from Scandinavia, the Baltics, Germany, Poland, and Ukraine. Like the immigrants, they found their place in small, close-knit communities that held on to the traditions of their homelands. And, as on the immigrants, America made its mark, changing them into something new and uniquely American. Over time, cheap, easy-to-work wheat flour replaced much of the rye, driving the rye content of some American "rye breads" to a mere 10% of total flour. To mask the change, the bakers loaded their breads with caraway.

No bread illustrates these changes as vividly as the dark brown American breads marketed as pumpernickel. In Europe, the word *pumpernickel* applies only to breads that bake for a minimum of 16 hours and whose dark color and sweet flavor develop naturally through the action of heat and enzymes on rye. Because slow baking takes time and uses valuable oven space, American bakers sweetened their everyday rye breads with sugar or molasses and colored them with cocoa, coffee, or burnt sugar (caramel coloring).

And so new breads were born that, despite all the compromises, held on to their Old World identities. New York Corn Rye (page 87) and Old Milwaukee Rye (page 99) may lack the intensity of Minsk Rye (page 267) and Bavarian Rye (page 219), but to eat them is to experience, in some small way, the traditions of the lands that spawned them.

Old-School Deli Rye

AMERICA When Americans think of rye bread, most envision the football-shaped rye breads that came from neighborhood Jewish or German bakeries. This old-style Jewish rye traces its roots to the breads of Ukraine and southern Poland, which produced both rye and wheat; thus, its lower rye percentage and twin virtues of rye's zesty flavor and wheat's ease of handling. This is the bread that sets the standard for authentic New York–style corned beef, pastrami, tongue, and Reuben sandwiches.

This traditional recipe, widely used in the Jewish bakeries of New York, features a two-stage sponge. The old-school bakers used either the milder white rye flour or medium rye flour—which I prefer—for its heartier flavor. I also like to add 15 g/0.50 oz./1 Tbs. or so of ground caraway seeds to perfume the dough, plus whole caraway or nigella seeds, both in the dough and as a topping, for extra crunch.

RYE %:	**39%**
STAGES:	**2-stage sponge, final dough**
LEAVEN:	**Rye sour, yeast**
START TO FINISH:	**26–28 hours**
HANDS-ON TIME:	**30–45 minutes**
YIELD:	**Two 1½ lb./608 g loaves**

STAGE 1 SPONGE (DAY 1, MORNING)

INGREDIENT	GRAMS	OUNCES	VOLUME	BAKER'S PERCENTAGE
White or medium rye flour	70	2.50	½ cup	100%
Warm (105°F/41°C) water	56	2.00	3 Tbs.	80%
Rye sour culture (see page 35)	14	0.50	1 Tbs.	20%

1. In the mixer bowl, mix the sponge ingredients by hand until blended. Cover and ferment at room temperature (68–72°F/20–22°C) overnight, 10–12 hours. The sponge will have doubled in bulk and have a clean sour smell.

STAGE 2 SPONGE (DAY 1, AFTERNOON)

INGREDIENT	GRAMS	OUNCES	VOLUME	BAKER'S PERCENTAGE
Stage 1 sponge	140	5.00	Use all	55%
White or medium rye flour	255	9.00	1¾ cups	100%
Warm (105°F/41°C) water	200	7.00	¾ cup + 2 Tbs.	78%

2. Add the Stage 2 ingredients, mix well, and ferment at room temperature until bubbly and doubled in bulk, 4–5 hours.

FINAL DOUGH (DAY 2, MORNING)

INGREDIENT	GRAMS	OUNCES	VOLUME
Stage 2 sponge	595	21.00	Use all
Warm (105°F/41°C) water	285	10.00	1¼ cups
First clear or high-gluten flour	480	17.00	4 cups
Salt	15	0.55	2¾ tsp.
Instant yeast	4	0.15	1 tsp.
Caraway seed, ground (optional)	15	0.55	1 Tbs.
Caraway or nigella seed (optional)	28	1.00	2 Tbs.
Flour and cornmeal for dusting	As needed		

3. Add the water to the Stage 2 sponge and stir until blended. Add the first clear or high-gluten flour, salt, and yeast, and the ground caraway and 15 g of the caraway seeds, if desired. Use the dough hook to mix at low (KA2) speed until the dough, which will be soft and moderately sticky, is well developed and leaves the sides of the bowl, 6–8 minutes. Cover and ferment at room temperature until doubled in bulk, 50–60 minutes.

4. Turn the dough onto a lightly floured work surface and knead back to its original volume, then divide it into two pieces, each weighing about 1½ lb./680 g. Shape each piece into a ball, then into a rounded oblong. Place the loaves on a cornmeal-dusted peel, if using a baking stone, or parchment-lined sheet pan that has been well-dusted with cornmeal. Cover the loaves and proof at room temperature until small cracks appear on the surface of the dough, 40–50 minutes.

recipe continues

5. Preheat the oven to 430°F/220°C with a steam pan (see page 76) and the baking surface in the middle. Slash each loaf three times crosswise to a depth of ¼–½ inch/0.6–1.25 cm, brush with water, and top with the additional seed if desired. Bake with steam for 10 minutes, then remove the steam pan, lower the temperature to 375°F/190°C, and bake until the loaves thump when tapped with a finger and the internal temperature is at least 198°F/92°C, 20–25 minutes.

GLAZE

INGREDIENT	GRAMS	OUNCES	VOLUME
Cornstarch	3	0.10	1 tsp.
Water	227	8.00	1 cup

6. While the bread is baking, dissolve the cornstarch in 28 ml/1.00 oz./2 Tbs. of the water and bring the remaining water to a boil. Stir the cornstarch mixture (it will settle) and pour it into the boiling water, stirring constantly until the glaze thickens to the consistency of honey, 3–4 minutes. Remove from the heat and let cool to room temperature. Transfer the loaves one at a time to a rack and immediately brush the crust with the glaze. Let cool thoroughly before slicing.

BAKER'S PERCENTAGES

INGREDIENT	G	%
TOTAL FLOUR	794	100.00%
First clear flour	482	60.71%
White rye flour	312	39.29%
Water	554	69.77%
Salt	17	2.14%
Instant yeast	4	0.50%
Caraway or nigella seed	14	1.79%
Rye sour culture	14	1.76%
TOTAL FORMULA	1,397	175.94%
Total flour prefermented	312	39.29%

Dakota Norwegian Rye

AMERICA This bread is yet another example of how traditional breads changed when they came across the Atlantic. I found this recipe in *Bread Lines*, the quarterly newsletter of the Bread Bakers Guild of America, and was both excited to have come across this representative of the Nordic rye tradition in America and intrigued with its adaptation to American tastes and agriculture.

North Dakota is rye country, and it's also wheat country—a rich land whose nineteenth-century Norwegian settlers come to life in Ole Rolvaag's classic family saga, *Giants in the Earth*, a book I've loved since I first read it in high school. This quintessentially American interpretation of a traditional rye bread was developed by Dakota Harvest Bakers in Grand Forks, North Dakota, for its Scandinavian-American customers who craved "bread like Nana used to make."

The bread is subtle, with a close and tender crumb and chewy crust. The first sensation is caraway: as Dakota Harvest Bakers' George Kelley told me, "The caraway seeds bring the distinct Norwegian flavor that, frankly, reminds the adults of their aquavit." The sour and sweetness are present, yet understated, as are the random nuggets of coarse rye that add interest to the chew. Enjoy this bread with liverwurst, Swiss cheese, summer sausage, or roast beef.

RYE %:	**29%**
STAGES:	**Sponge, final dough**
LEAVEN:	**Rye sour culture, yeast**
START TO FINISH:	**16–20 hours**
HANDS-ON TIME:	**30–35 minutes**
YIELD:	**One 2¼ lb./1.0 kg loaf**

SPONGE (DAY 1, EVENING)

INGREDIENT	GRAMS	OUNCES	VOLUME	BAKER'S PERCENTAGE
Whole-wheat flour	50	1.75	⅜ cup	33%
Fine rye meal	50	1.75	¼ cup	33%
Coarse rye meal or rye chops	50	1.75	⅓ cup	33%
Warm (105°F/41°C) water	150	5.30	⅝ cup	100%
Rye sour culture (see page 35)	40	1.40	3¼ Tbs.	27%

recipe continues

The hardy Norsemen who settled America's northern plains brought their breads with them. **Dakota Norwegian Rye**, shown here with kielbasa, is a modern interpretation of those traditional breads that represents the best of the Norwegian American baking tradition.

1. Mix the sponge ingredients by hand until incorporated, cover, and ferment at room temperature (68–72°F/20–22°C) overnight, 12–15 hours. The sponge will be very bubbly, have a clean sour smell, and will have doubled in volume.

FINAL DOUGH (DAY 2, MORNING)

INGREDIENT	GRAMS	OUNCES	VOLUME
Bread flour	400	14.10	2⅞ cups
Medium rye flour	80	2.80	⅝ cup
Salt	10	0.35	1⅔ tsp.
Instant yeast	5	0.15	1 tsp.
Dark brown sugar, packed	40	1.40	3 Tbs.
Sponge	340	12.00	Use all
Warm (105°F/41°C) water	200	7.05	⅚ cup
Malt or white vinegar	20	0.70	4 tsp.
Caraway seed	5	0.20	2½ tsp.
Flour for dusting	As needed		

2. In the mixer, combine the flours, salt, yeast, and sugar, then add the sponge, water, vinegar, and caraway seed. Use the dough hook and mix at low (KA2) speed until the dough comes together into a soft, sticky mass, 6–8 minutes. Cover and ferment at room temperature until doubled in volume, 1½–2 hours.

3. Turn the dough, which will have become more elastic and easier to work, onto a lightly floured work surface and shape it into a rounded oblong loaf 14–16 inches/35–40 cm long. Place on a well-floured peel, if using a baking stone, or on a parchment-lined sheet pan, cover, and proof at room temperature until doubled in volume, 45–60 minutes.

4. Preheat the oven to 430°F/220°C with a steam pan (see page 76) and the baking surface in the middle. Use a sharp knife or razor blade to make three diagonal slashes to a depth of ¼–½ inch/0.6–1.25 cm. Bake with steam for 15 minutes, then remove the steam pan and continue baking until the loaf thumps when tapped with a finger and the internal temperature is at least 198°F/92°C, 30–35 minutes. Transfer to a rack and cool thoroughly before slicing.

recipe continues

BAKER'S PERCENTAGES

INGREDIENT	G	%
TOTAL FLOUR	630	100.00%
Bread flour	400	63.49%
Medium rye flour	80	12.70%
Whole-wheat flour	50	7.94%
Fine rye meal	50	7.94%
Coarse rye meal	50	7.94%
Water	350	55.56%
Salt	10	1.59%
Instant yeast	5	0.76%
Brown sugar	40	6.35%
Vinegar	20	3.17%
Caraway seed	5	0.79%
Rye sour culture	40	6.35%
TOTAL FORMULA	1,100	174.57%
Total flour prefermented	150	23.81%

New York Corn Rye

AMERICA *Kornbroyt*, as my Yiddish-speaking grandparents called it, was always a special treat for me growing up. The loaves were large, often weighing as much as 3 or 4 pounds, so the bakers sold it by the pound in half and quarter loaves that we cut into thick slices. The flavor was a blend of sour and caraway, the crumb dense and chewy. Grandma Annie would garnish it with a schmear of chicken fat (*schmaltz*), fried onions, and a little salt. Bubbe Becky liked it rubbed lightly with the cut end of a garlic clove. I like it with corned beef, pastrami, or pickled tongue.

Note that although the ingredients are essentially the same as for the Jewish Deli Rye, *kornbroyt* is more technically demanding in that the dough is far stickier than for Old-School Deli Rye (page 80) and baking takes place right after the bulk ferment, with no proofing of the loaves.

For anyone whose memories of Jewish corn rye are rich with the associations of family and traditions, or who craves the taste of a lost world, here's a great recipe.

RYE %:	**35%**
STAGES:	**Sponge, final dough**
LEAVEN:	**Rye sour culture, yeast**
START TO FINISH:	**12–14 hours**
HANDS-ON TIME:	**30–45 minutes**
YIELD:	**One 3 lb./1.35 kg loaf**

SPONGE (DAY 1, EVENING)

INGREDIENT	GRAMS	OUNCES	VOLUME	BAKER'S PERCENTAGE
White or medium rye flour	285	10.00	2¾ cups	100%
Warm (105°F/41°C) water	227	8.00	1 cup	80%
Salt	3	0.10	¼ tsp.	1%
Rye sour culture (see page 35)	57	2.00	¼ cup	20%

1. Mix the sponge ingredients by hand until incorporated, cover, and ferment at room temperature (68–72°F/20–22°C) overnight, 10–12 hours. The sponge will be very bubbly, have a clean sour smell, and will have doubled in volume.

recipe continues

FINAL DOUGH (DAY 2, MORNING)

INGREDIENT	GRAMS	OUNCES	VOLUME
Sponge	572	20.15	Use all
First clear or high-gluten flour	540	19.00	3⅞ cups
Warm (105°F/41°C) water	270	9.50	1 cup + 3 Tbs.
Salt	6	0.25	1 tsp.
Instant yeast	18	0.65	1½ Tbs.
Caraway seed (optional)	13	0.45	2 Tbs.
Cornmeal for dusting	As needed		

2. Add the sponge, flour, warm water, salt, yeast, and caraway seed to the stand mixer, then use the dough hook at low (KA2) speed, scraping down the bowl as necessary, to mix until the dough comes together into a soft, sticky mass, 6–8 minutes. Pour about 30 ml/1 oz./2 Tbs. water into a separate bowl, then use a plastic dough scraper and wet hands to transfer the dough. Turn the dough to moisten all surfaces, cover, and ferment at room temperature until doubled in volume, 45–60 minutes.

3. Turn the dough onto a peel or parchment-lined sheet pan dusted generously with cornmeal and use wet hands to gently shape it into a thick disk, taking care not to disturb the dough any more than necessary. Brush the crust with water and sprinkle with caraway seed if desired.

4. Preheat the oven to 450°F/230°C with a steam pan (see page 76) and the baking surface in the middle. Bake for 10 minutes with steam, then remove the steam pan, lower the temperature to 350°F/175°C, and bake until the loaf thumps when tapped with a finger and the internal temperature is at least 198°F/92°C, 75–90 minutes.

GLAZE

INGREDIENT	GRAMS	OUNCES	VOLUME
Cornstarch	3	0.10	1 tsp.
Water	227	8.00	1 cup

5. While the bread is baking, dissolve the cornstarch in 28 ml/1.00 oz./2 Tbs. of water and bring the remaining water to a boil. Stir the cornstarch mixture (it will settle) and pour it into the boiling water, stirring constantly until the glaze thickens to the consistency of honey, 3–4 minutes. Remove from the heat and let cool to room temperature. Transfer the loaf to a rack and immediately brush the crust with the glaze. Let cool thoroughly before slicing.

BAKER'S PERCENTAGES

INGREDIENT	G	%
TOTAL FLOUR	824	100.00%
First clear flour	539	65.40%
Rye flour	285	34.60%
Water	496	60.23%
Salt	18	2.24%
Instant yeast	6	0.69%
Caraway seed	13	1.55%
Rye sour culture	57	6.88%
TOTAL FORMULA	1,413	171.59%
Total flour prefermented	285	34.60%

Boston Brown Bread is an All-American classic combining rye, whole wheat, cornmeal, and molasses into a dense, bittersweet loaf that's the traditional accompaniment to Boston Baked Beans.

Boston Brown Bread

AMERICA When the first English colonists came to America, it was rye they carried. Rye and Indian bread, made with native maize, water, salt, and perhaps a bit of molasses to add sweetness, quickly became a mainstay of the New England diet. Over decades and centuries, as the colonies prospered, declared their independence, and expanded west and south, a growing supply of low-cost wheat transformed that coarse rye and Indian bread into the more refined Boston Brown Bread that New Englanders eat to this day.

Technically a quick bread, Boston Brown Bread steams slowly at the low temperatures typical of a fireplace nook or banked stone oven. The bread—a steamed pudding, really—is dense and tender with a grainy mouthfeel of stone-ground cornmeal and whole-wheat flour. The strong coffee, caramel, and acid notes of the molasses dominate the flavor profile.

There are many recipes for Boston Brown Bread. Most call for equal amounts of rye, corn, and wheat. This one, which contains 40% rye and about 25% wheat, dates from 1903 and recalls the tastes and textures of an earlier time. Eat it as the traditional accompaniment to Boston baked beans.

RYE %:	**40%**
STAGES:	**Straight dough**
LEAVEN:	**Baking soda**
START TO FINISH:	**3½ hours**
HANDS-ON TIME:	**15 minutes**
YIELD:	**One 2¼ lb./1 kg loaf**

recipe continues

DOUGH

INGREDIENT	GRAMS	OUNCES	VOLUME	BAKER'S PERCENTAGE
Fine rye meal or medium rye flour	185	6.55	1½ cups	39.78%
Yellow cornmeal	160	5.65	1 cup	34.41%
Whole-wheat flour	120	4.25	1 cup	25.81%
Whole milk	425	15.00	1¾ cups	91.40%
Salt	6	0.20	1 tsp.	1.29%
Baking soda	4	0.15	1 tsp.	0.86%
Unsulphured dark molasses	255	9.00	¾ cup	54.84%
TOTAL FORMULA	1,155	40.80		248.39%
Total flour	465	16.45		100.00%
Vegetable shortening for pan	As needed			

1. Mix all of the ingredients into a smooth batter by hand or machine and place in a well-greased 8½-by-4½-by-3-inch/22-by-12-by-8 cm loaf pan.

2. Seal the pan tightly with greased aluminum foil and bake in a preheated 200°F/95°C oven for 3 hours. Let cool in the pan.

Jewish Bakery Pumpernickel

By the end of World War II the dense European rye breads that came to America during the Great Immigration half a century earlier had all but disappeared from bakery shelves. To be sure, those shelves still held dark brown breads called " pumpernickel," but they were pumpernickel in name only. In place of the rye in the immigrant breads, the bakers substituted cheaper, easier-to-work wheat, driving the rye content in some cases to a bare 10% of the total flour. Instead of unlocking the rye's hidden sweetness, the bakers sweetened their loaves with sugar or corn syrup and darkened them with molasses, coffee, or burnt sugar (caramel color). To mask the disappearance of the rye, they loaded their loaves with caraway seed.

In the process, a new American bread was born—Jewish bakery pumpernickel. This version, which contains more than 40% coarse rye meal and no added sweeteners, harks back to an earlier age and represents, in my opinion, the best of class. Substitute it anywhere you'd use Old-School Deli Rye (see page 80).

RYE %:	**42%**
STAGES:	**2-stage sponge, final dough**
LEAVEN:	**Rye sour culture, yeast**
START TO FINISH:	**26–28 hours**
HANDS-ON TIME:	**35–45 minutes**
YIELD:	**Two 1½ lb./650 g loaves**

STAGE 1 SPONGE (DAY 1, MORNING)

INGREDIENT	GRAMS	OUNCES	VOLUME	BAKER'S PERCENTAGE
Coarse rye meal	127	4.50	¾ cup + 1 Tbs.	100%
Warm (105°F/41°C) water	105	3.70	½ cup less 2 tsp.	83%
Rye sour culture (see page 35)	13	0.45	1 Tbs.	10%

1. Mix the sponge ingredients by hand until incorporated, cover, and ferment at room temperature (68–72°F/20–22°C) for 6–8 hours. The sponge will have a clean sour smell and will have expanded only slightly.

recipe continues

STAGE 2 SPONGE (DAY 1, AFTERNOON)

INGREDIENT	GRAMS	OUNCES	VOLUME	BAKER'S PERCENTAGE
Stage 1 sponge	245	8.65	Use all	100%
Coarse rye meal	245	8.65	1½ cups	100%
Warm (105°F/41°C) water	327	12.00	1½ cups	133%

2. Combine the Stage 2 ingredients with the Stage 1 sponge, cover, and ferment at room temperature for 4–5 hours, then refrigerate overnight.

FINAL DOUGH (DAY 2, MORNING)

INGREDIENT	GRAMS	OUNCES	VOLUME
Caramel color (see page 97)	30	1.05	1½ Tbs.
Warm (105°F/41°C) water	100	3.50	½ cup less 1 Tbs.
Stage 2 sponge	817	29.30	Use all
First clear or high gluten flour	510	18.00	3½ cups
Salt	16	0.6	1 Tbs.
Instant yeast	7	0.25	1¾ tsp.
Flour for dusting	As needed		
Yellow cornmeal for dusting	As needed		

3. Dissolve the caramel color in the water, add to the sponge, and mix by hand until the color is uniform. Add the flour, salt, and yeast and use the dough hook at low (KA2) speed to mix until the dough, which will be stiff, with no obvious gluten development, becomes smooth, and evenly colored, 6–8 minutes. Cover and ferment at room temperature until the dough has expanded to 1½ times its original volume, about 1 hour.

4. Turn the dough onto a lightly floured work surface and knead back to its original volume. Divide into two pieces, each weighing about 700 g/25 oz., and roll each piece into a ball, then shape into a rounded oval about 10 inches/25 cm long and 4–5 inches/10–13 cm wide. Set the loaves seam side down on a peel, if using a baking stone, or parchment-lined sheet pan that has been dusted generously with cornmeal. Cover and proof at room temperature until the surface of the dough shows cracks, 45–60 minutes.

5. Preheat the oven to 400°F/205°C with a steam pan (see page 76) and the baking surface in the middle. Brush or spray the loaves with water, slash two or three times crosswise to a depth of ¼–½ inch/0.6–1.25 cm, and bake with steam for 10 minutes. Remove the steam pan, lower the oven temperature to 350°F/175°C, and bake until the loaf thumps when tapped with a finger and the internal temperature is at least 198°F/92°C, 35–40 minutes.

GLAZE

INGREDIENT	GRAMS	OUNCES	VOLUME
Cornstarch	3	0.10	1 tsp.
Water	227	8.00	1 cup

6. While the bread is baking, dissolve the cornstarch in 28 ml/1.00 oz./2 Tbs. of the water and bring the remaining water to a boil. Stir the cornstarch mixture (it will settle) and pour it into the boiling water, stirring constantly until the glaze thickens to the consistency of honey, 3–4 minutes. Remove from the heat and let cool to room temperature. Transfer the loaves one at a time to a rack and immediately brush the crust with the glaze. Let cool thoroughly before slicing.

Variations

SEEDED PUMPERNICKEL Add 7–14 g/0.25–0.5 oz./ 1–2 Tbs. whole caraway or nigella seeds in Step 2. Just before putting loaves in the oven but before slashing, spray or brush with warm water and sprinkle the tops of the loaves generously with whole seeds. Bake as directed.

ONION PUMPERNICKEL Soak 15 g/0.5 oz./ ¼ cup dehydrated onion flakes in 1 cup boiling water. Drain and add the onions to the final dough.

RAISIN PUMPERNICKEL Soak 85 g/3.0 oz./ ½ cup raisins in 227 ml /8.0 oz./1 cup boiling water, drain, and add them after the final dough has come together, mixing just enough to distribute them evenly through the dough.

MARBLE RYE In Europe, the poor often dressed up their dark breads with a thin layer of lighter dough. This tradition is reflected in marble rye, which always has the light rye layer on the outside. To make

recipe continues

marble rye, prepare one half recipe each of Old-School Deli Rye (page 80) and Jewish Bakery Pumpernickel. Divide each into two pieces, then place the pumpernickel dough on the deli rye dough, flatten with your hands, and roll toward you into a rounded oblong. Bake as directed.

BAKER'S PERCENTAGES

INGREDIENT	G	%
TOTAL FLOUR	882	100.00%
First clear flour	510	57.84%
Coarse rye meal	372	42.16%
Water	489	55.39%
Salt	17	1.93%
Instant yeast	7	0.80%
Caramel color	30	3.40%
Rye sour culture	13	1.47%
TOTAL FORMULA	1,438	162.99%
Total flour prefermented	372	42.16%

HOW TO MAKE CARAMEL COLOR

Caramel color, the professionals' coloring agent of choice, is available commercially but is hard to find in retail sizes. This bakers' recipe uses sugar, water, and cream of tartar, which prevents the sugar from recrystallizing, and makes about 225 g/8 oz.—enough to color 15–20 loaves of pumpernickel. If you need less coloring, reduce the ingredients proportionally.

INGREDIENT	GRAMS	OUNCES	VOLUME	BAKER'S PERCENTAGE
Sugar	175	6.00	¾ cup	100%
Water	55	2.00	¼ cup	33%
Cream of tartar	2	0.08	¼ tsp.	1%
Boiling water	56	2.00	¼ cup	33%

1. Combine the sugar and water in a heavy saucepan over low heat until the sugar dissolves completely.

2. Raise the heat to medium, cover the pan, bring to a boil, and boil for 2 minutes.

3. Stir in the cream of tartar and continue boiling, uncovered, until the syrup turns nearly black, about 10 minutes. Remove from the heat and slowly add the boiling water, stirring with a long-handled spoon or whisk (the syrup will spatter violently when the water hits it), until the mixture reaches the consistency of honey, 2 to 3 minutes. Cool to room temperature. Stored in glass or plastic it will keep indefinitely.

The Polish and German immigrants who gave Milwaukee its character also produced **Old Milwaukee Rye**, a Central European hybrid that combines the astringency of caraway with the sweet and dark coffee notes of molasses.

Old Milwaukee Rye

AMERICA Until I arrived in Madison, Wisconsin, in the mid-1960s to attend grad school, my only experience of rye bread was with the Jewish ryes, corn ryes, and caramel-colored pumpernickels of the Jewish bakeries in my native New York. So when I first tasted the ubiquitous Milwaukee rye, I was both intrigued with its sweetness and skeptical that people had the nerve to call it rye bread when everyone knew that the only real rye bread was the stuff I'd grown up with.

What I didn't know and hardly thought about was the bread's pedigree. Just as Eastern European Jews brought the rye breads of Russia, Poland, and Ukraine to New York, so did the Poles and Germans who gave Milwaukee its character bring their sweet, spicy rye breads. It didn't take long for this bread to grow on me, especially paired with Wisconsin favorites like liverwurst and Polish mustard, Wisconsin cheddar cheese, and summer sausage.

RYE %:	**45%**
STAGES:	**Sponge, final dough**
LEAVEN:	**Rye sour culture, yeast**
START TO FINISH:	**10–15 hours**
HANDS-ON TIME:	**25–30 minutes**
YIELD:	**Two 1½ lb./680 g loaves**

SPONGE (DAY 1, EVENING)

INGREDIENT	GRAMS	OUNCES	VOLUME	BAKER'S PERCENTAGE
Medium rye flour	180	6.35	1⅜ cups	100%
Warm (105°F/41°C) water	260	9.15	1⅛ cups	144%
Rye sour culture (see page 35)	48	1.70	¼ cup	27%

1. Mix the sponge ingredients by hand until incorporated, cover, and ferment at room temperature (68–72°F/20–22°C) overnight, 10–12 hours. The sponge will be very bubbly, have a clean sour smell, and will have doubled in volume.

recipe continues

The Essential Loaf:
France and Spain

EVEN though very few people identify France and Spain with rye bread, both countries have a strong historical connection to the unruly weed. In the Middle Ages, rye was an important bread cereal throughout France, from Brittany and Normandy in the far Northwest to the Alpine foothills of Provence in the Southeast and across the midsection of the country, where it grew abundantly on the Massif Central, the vast mountain range that dominates south central France. Rye also thrived in the high elevation and cool climate of Castile-León[61] and the sandy coastal plain of Galicia, both in the extreme Northwest of the Iberian Peninsula.

Although distant from each other, both France and Spain share a minimalist baking tradition that's reflected in their breads. Their rye and rye-wheat loaves are made with flour, water or other liquid, yeast, and salt only.[*]

In that simplicity, however, resides a world of flavor—from the dense sweetness of the Breton Folded Rye (page 105) and Auvergne Rye-Wheat Boule (page 111) to the apple-fragrant Normandy Apple Cider Rye (page 115) and the delicate sour and tender, open crumb of the Galician Rye Bread (page 107).

[*] The exception is Spiced Honey Rye (see page 117), a celebration bread that reflects the tradition the Italians call *cucina povera*, the cooking of the poor—that is, embellishing the ordinary with costly ingredients to elevate it into something special.

Breton Folded Rye. Instead of using sour sponges to retard starch attack (see page 32), the rye bakers of Brittany simply accelerated the baking time line to produce a tender, tight-crumbed loaf that features the natural sweetness of rye and milk, and wants nothing more than a light film of sweet butter.

Breton Folded Rye

Pain de Seigle Plié

FRANCE This bread, which takes its name from the three folds that form the finished loaf, is a great illustration of French practicality. Rather than using the techniques we find elsewhere to counter rye's idiosyncrasies, the bakers of Brittany simply did an end run around them. By compressing the fermentation and baking time into as tight a window as possible—only 30 minutes for each—they effectively robbed the amylase enzymes of the time needed to launch their starch attack. The result is a tight-crumbed yet very tender country loaf that brings out the natural sweetness of rye and milk and finishes with a subtle extended tang.

RYE %:	**64%**
STAGES:	**Straight dough**
LEAVEN:	**Yeast**
START TO FINISH:	**2 hours**
HANDS-ON TIME:	**20–25 minutes**
YIELD:	**One 1¾ lb./800 g loaf**

DOUGH

INGREDIENT	GRAMS	OUNCES	VOLUME	BAKER'S PERCENTAGE
Medium rye flour	320	11.30	2½ cups	64.00%
AP flour	180	6.35	1½ cups	36.00%
Whole milk, at room temperature (68–72°F/20–22°C)	320	11.30	1⅓ cups	64.00%
Instant yeast	8	0.30	¾ Tbs.	1.60%
Salt	9	0.30	1½ tsp.	1.80%
Sugar	9	0.30	2 tsp.	1.80%
TOTAL FORMULA	846	29.85		169.20%
Total flour	500	17.85		100.00%
Flour for dusting	As needed			

recipe continues

1. Combine all the ingredients in the mixer and use the dough hook at low (KA2) speed to mix until the dough comes together and leaves the sides of the bowl, 6–8 minutes.

2. Turn the dough onto a lightly floured surface—it will be very stiff and only slightly sticky—and form it into a ball, then flatten it into a disk 8–10 inches/20–25 cm in diameter and 1–1½ inches/2.5–4.0 cm thick. Use a straightedge to make three ½-inch/1.25 cm deep depressions in the dough in the shape of an equilateral triangle with its points at the edges of the dough.

3. Fold the sides up along the depressions and pinch the corners together, forming a triangle of dough. Place the loaf on a lightly floured peel, if using a baking stone, or a parchment-lined sheet pan. Cover and proof at room temperature (68–72°F/20–22°C) until the surface shows cracks or broken bubbles, 30–45 minutes.

4. Preheat the oven to 430°F/220°C with the baking surface in the upper third. Bake until the loaf thumps when tapped with a finger and the internal temperature is at least 198°F/92°C, 30–35 minutes. Transfer to a rack and cool thoroughly before slicing.

Galician Rye Bread

Pan Gallego de Centeno

`SPAIN` There are many variations of *pan Gallego*, each with a distinctive shape and composition. This one comes from Ourense, in south central Galicia, not far from the Portuguese border. To the Spaniards, the full, round loaf, topped with a spherical knot of dough, like a brioche, resembles a female breast, earning it the name *moña* ("female mannequin").

This bread starts with a rye sponge to which bread flour, salt, a touch of yeast, and a large amount of water—85% of total flour weight—are added, producing a very wet, very loose dough. The dough rests for 20 minutes to initiate gluten formation, followed by an unusually long 30 minutes of machine kneading to strengthen the gluten. The result is a crusty, rustic loaf with a surprisingly open crumb. Bright sour dominates, supported by the spicy sweetness of wheat and rye.

This is a great all-around table bread but is at its finest in *pa amb tomàquet*, sometimes called "Catalan bruschetta." To make it, toast a slice of Galician Rye, rub it with a clove of garlic, and then grate half of a tomato on the toast, until the pulp and juice are fully absorbed and only the skin remains. Top with a sprinkling of kosher salt and a few drops of extra virgin olive oil. Wash it down with a glass of Spanish Rioja.

RYE %:	*44%*
STAGES:	**Sponge, final dough**
LEAVEN:	**Rye sour culture, yeast**
START TO FINISH:	**13–16 hours**
HANDS-ON TIME:	**45–50 minutes**
YIELD:	**One 2 lb./910 g loaf**

SPONGE

INGREDIENT	GRAMS	OUNCES	VOLUME	BAKER'S PERCENTAGE
Medium rye flour	170	6.00	1⅓ cups	100%
Water	170	6.00	¾ cup	100%
Rye sour culture (see page 35)	17	0.60	4 tsp.	10%

recipe continues

Galician Rye Bread. One doesn't think of Spain as rye country, but this traditional boule from Galicia in the far northwest uses an extremely wet dough and long ferment that produce this flavorful, open-crumbed bread.

1. In the mixer bowl, mix the sponge ingredients by hand until incorporated, cover and ferment at room temperature (68–72°F/20–22°C) overnight, 10–12 hours. The sponge will be very bubbly, have a clean sour smell, and will have doubled in volume.

FINAL DOUGH

INGREDIENT	GRAMS	OUNCES	VOLUME
Water at room temperature	285	10.05	1¼ cups
Bread flour	300	10.60	2⅛ cups
Rye sponge	357	12.60	Use all
Medium rye flour	65	2.30	½ cup
Salt	9	0.30	1½ tsp.
Instant yeast	1	0.05	⅓ tsp.
Flour for dusting	As needed		

2. Add the water and 50 g/1.80 oz./⅓ cup of the bread flour to the sponge and hand-mix until it forms a slurry. Add the remaining bread flour and the rye flour and use the paddle to mix at low (KA2) speed until the dough is evenly hydrated, 3–4 minutes. Cover the dough and let it rest for 15–20 minutes.

3. Add the salt and yeast and use the dough hook to mix at low (KA2) speed until the the gluten is very well developed, 30–35 minutes. Cover and ferment at room temperature until doubled in volume, 2–2½ hours.

4. Turn the dough onto a generously floured work surface and gently form it into a ball by folding it toward you, rotating 90 degrees and repeating until the bottom surface is smooth. Flip the dough, pinch a golf-ball-sized piece of dough from the center of the loaf and stretch it upward without separating it from the loaf, then form a depression and place the ball of dough inside. Place on a parchment-lined sheet pan or, if using a baking stone, on a well-floured peel. Cover and proof at room temperature for 10 minutes.

5. Preheat the oven to 430°F/220°C with the baking surface in the middle and a steam pan (see page 76) on a lower shelf. Bake with steam for 15 minutes, then remove the steam pan and lower the temperature to 390°F/200°C. Bake until the crust is golden brown, the loaf thumps when tapped with a finger, and the internal temperature is at least 198°F/92°C, 35–40 minutes. Transfer to a rack and cool thoroughly before slicing.

recipe continues

BAKER'S PERCENTAGES

INGREDIENT	G	%
TOTAL FLOUR	535	100.00%
Bread flour	300	56.07%
Medium rye flour	235	43.93%
Water	455	85.05%
Salt	9	1.68%
Instant yeast	1	0.19%
Rye sour culture	17	3.18%
TOTAL FORMULA	1,017	190.10%
Total flour prefermented	170	31.78%

Auvergne Rye-Wheat Boule

Pain de Méteil d'Auvergne

FRANCE For centuries rye was one of France's principal grains. Even after wheat displaced it in most of the country, Brittany, Normandy, and the mountain range, the Massif Central, that dominates the center of the country, where rye continues to thrive, never completely lost their taste for their traditional breads. This bread, made of the 50-50 blend of wheat and rye known as *méteil*, is an outlier in the wheaten world of French baking but one that offers the rich sourdough flavors and rustic mouthfeel of an earlier age.

This *pain de méteil* uses both rye and wheat sponges that are refrigerated overnight to unlock the hidden flavors of the flours. To bring out even more flavor, the final dough undergoes a bulk fermentation that lasts for 2–2½ hours, along with stretch-and-folds to develop the gluten. The high-temperature bake with 15 minutes of steam produces a dense yet very tender crumb wrapped in a thick, crisp crust. In all, this is a distinctively French rustic loaf that features both the earthiness of the rye and the sweetness of wheat, with just a touch of sour. In Auvergne, this is the bread that accompanies *potée Auvergnate*, a stew of cabbage, potatoes, and pork; *coq au vin*; and strong-flavored cheeses like Cantal, Sarasson, and Saint-Nectaire.

RYE %:	**50%**
STAGES:	**Rye sponge, wheat sponge, final dough**
LEAVEN:	**Rye sour culture, yeast**
START TO FINISH:	**14–18 hours (22–28 hours with optional sponge retardation)**
HANDS-ON TIME:	**45–60 minutes**
YIELD:	**One 2 lb./910 g loaf**

RYE SPONGE (DAY 1, EVENING)

INGREDIENT	GRAMS	OUNCES	VOLUME	BAKER'S PERCENTAGE
Medium rye flour	95	3.35	¾ cup	100%
Warm (105°F/41°C) water	95	3.35	⅜ cup	100%
Rye sour culture (see page 35)	10	0.35	2½ tsp.	11%

recipe continues

1. Mix the sponge ingredients by hand until incorporated, cover, and ferment at room temperature (68–72°F/20–22°C) overnight, 10–12 hours. The sponge will be very bubbly, have a clean sour smell, and will have doubled in volume.

WHEAT SPONGE (DAY 1, EVENING)

INGREDIENT	GRAMS	OUNCES	VOLUME	BAKER'S PERCENTAGE
AP flour	140	4.95	1 cup	100%
Warm (105°F/41°C) water	140	4.95	⅝ cup	100%
Instant yeast	1	0.05	⅓ tsp.	1%

2. In a separate bowl, mix the wheat sponge ingredients by hand until incorporated, cover, and ferment at room temperature for 10–12 hours or overnight. The sponge will be very bubbly and at least double its original bulk.

Optional step: To bring out even more of the flour's hidden flavors, refrigerate both sponges for 8–10 hours or overnight and remove from the refrigerator 1–2 hours before mixing the final dough to take out the chill.

FINAL DOUGH (DAY 2, MORNING)

INGREDIENT	GRAMS	OUNCES	VOLUME
Medium rye flour	205	7.25	1⅝ cups
AP flour	160	5.65	1¼ cups
Salt	12	0.40	2 tsp.
Wheat sponge	281	9.90	Use all
Rye sponge	200	7.05	Use all
Warm (105°F/41°C) water	160	5.65	⅔ cup
Flour for dusting	As needed		

3. Combine the flours and salt in the mixer. Dissolve the sponges in the water, add to the dry ingredients, and use the dough hook at low (KA2) speed to mix until the dough cleans the side of the bowl and gathers around the hook, 6–8 minutes.

4. Transfer the dough, which will be firm and slightly sticky, to a lightly floured work surface, cover, and ferment at room temperature. Stretch and fold the dough after 40 and 80 minutes by pulling out the four corners and folding them in toward the center, continuing to ferment until doubled in volume, 2–2½ hours.

5. Using lightly floured hands, gently shape the dough into a ball, cover, and let rest for 15 minutes at room temperature to relax the gluten. Give the dough its final shaping into a football-shaped loaf, then place it on a well-floured peel, if using a baking stone, or a parchment-lined sheet pan. Cover and proof at room temperature until the loaf doubles in volume, 75–90 minutes.

6. Preheat the oven to 480°F/250°C with a steam pan (see page 76) and the baking surface in the middle. Slash the dough once lengthwise to a depth of ¼–½ inch/0.6–1.25 cm and bake with steam for 15 minutes. Remove the steam pan, lower the oven temperature to 445°F/230°C, and bake until the crust is a deep brown, thumps when tapped with a finger, and the internal temperature is at least 198°F/92°C, 30–35 minutes. Transfer to a rack and cool thoroughly before slicing.

BAKER'S PERCENTAGES

INGREDIENT	G	%
TOTAL FLOUR	600	100.00%
Medium rye flour	300	50.00%
AP flour	300	50.00%
Water	395	65.83%
Salt	12	2.00%
Instant yeast	1	0.17%
Rye sour culture	10	1.67%
TOTAL FORMULA	1,018	169.67%
Total flour prefermented	235	39.17%
Total wheat flour prefermented	140	23.33%
Total rye flour prefermented	95	15.83%

Normandy is France's apple region, and this traditional **Apple Cider Rye** substitutes hard cider for water, giving the finished boule a strong apple fragrance and a sweet-spicy flavor profile.

Normandy Apple Cider Rye

Pain au Cidre

FRANCE Normandy is known for its apples. Its Calvados is the yardstick by which other apple brandies are measured, and its *tartes-Tatins* are world class. Apples also play a prominent role in this bread, which uses fermented apple cider in place of water.

Like so many French rye breads, yeast is the leavening agent; apple cider provides the acidity needed to slow the enzymatic degradation of the rye starches, aka "starch attack" (see page 32). The long kneading—nearly 20 minutes—produces a soft and very sticky dough. It also develops the gluten in the wheat flour, which strengthens the bread's structure even though wheat makes up less than 30% of the total flour.

The bread is open-crumbed and tender, with a strong apple fragrance and a flavor profile that marries the sweetness of cider and the spiciness of the rye. Try this bread with traditional Norman specialties, such as Camembert cheese, roast lamb, and poached oysters with apples and mushrooms.

RYE %:	**71%**
STAGES:	**Straight dough**
LEAVEN:	**Yeast**
START TO FINISH:	**3½–4 hours**
HANDS-ON TIME:	**20 minutes**
YIELD:	**Two 1½ lb./700 g loaves**

recipe continues

DOUGH

INGREDIENT	GRAMS	OUNCES	VOLUME	BAKER'S PERCENTAGE
AP flour	350	12.35	2¾ cups	66.67%
Fine rye meal	150	5.30	⅞ cup	28.57%
Warm (105°F/41°C) water	310	10.95	1¼ cups	59.05%
Rye sour culture (see page 35)	50	1.75	¼ cup	9.52%
Instant yeast	4	0.15	1 ¼ tsp.	0.76%
Salt	14	0.50	2¼ tsp.	2.67%
Vegetable oil	14	0.50	1 Tbs.	2.67%
Flour for dusting	As needed			
Finely shredded red or green cabbage	140	4.95	2 cups	26.67%
Chopped onion, sautéed until translucent	50	1.75	¼ cup	9.52%
Chopped fresh parsley, dill, or chives	15	0.55	¼ cup	2.86%
TOTAL FORMULA	1,097	38.75		208.95%
Total flour	500	17.65		100.00%

1. In the mixer, combine the flour, rye meal, warm water, rye sour culture, yeast, salt, and oil. Use the dough hook at low (KA2) speed to mix until the dough comes together and leaves the sides of the bowl, 6–8 minutes.

2. Turn the dough onto a well-floured surface and gently knead in the cabbage, sautéed onions, and fresh herbs. Form the dough into a ball, place it in a lightly oiled bowl, cover, and ferment at room temperature (68–72°F/20–22°C) until the dough has visibly expanded, 20–30 minutes.

3. Return the dough to the work surface, divide it into two pieces, each weighing about 545 g/19 oz., and shape into round or oblong loaves. Place on a well-floured peel, if using a baking stone, or a parchment-lined sheet pan, cover, and ferment at room temperature until the dough shows broken bubbles or fine cracks, 30–45 minutes.

4. Preheat the oven to 410°F/210°C with the baking surface in the middle. Slash the loaves diagonally two or three times to a depth of ¼–½ inch/0.6–1.25 cm. Reduce the heat to 375°F/190°C and bake until the loaf thumps when tapped with a finger and the internal temperature is at least 198°F/92°C, 40–45 minutes (the crust will not brown deeply but will remain a pale tan). Transfer to a rack and cool thoroughly before slicing.

Danish Rye Bread

Rågbrød

`DENMARK` *Smørrebrød*, open-faced sandwiches, are a Danish national passion. Depending on the topping—anything from pickled herring and smoked salmon to liver *pâte* and roast beef—they can be built on an array of rye breads ranging from very sour to very sweet.

This Danish rye bread is one of the sweet ones, its flavors brought out by a long scald and the generous addition of light molasses syrup. The combination of sunflower seeds and flaxseed, coarse rye meal, and cracked wheat gives it a chewy, rustic texture and an engaging nutty flavor. This bread goes wonderfully with strong cheeses like Danish blue and aged cheddar, as well as cured meats and fish.

RYE %:	**75%**
STAGES:	**Scald, final dough**
LEAVEN:	**Yeast**
START TO FINISH:	**18–22 hours**
HANDS-ON TIME:	**30–40 minutes**
YIELD:	**One 4 lb./1.80 kg loaf**

SCALD (DAY 1, EVENING)

INGREDIENT	GRAMS	OUNCES	VOLUME	BAKER'S PERCENTAGE
Medium rye flour	240	8.50	1⅞ cups	100%
Boiling water	400	14.10	1⅔ cups	167%
Salt	27	0.95	1½ Tbs.	11%
Sunflower seeds	160	5.65	1⅛ cups	67%
Flaxseed	40	1.40	¼ cup	17%

1. Combine the scald ingredients in a bowl and cover. Let cool to room temperature (68–72°F/20–22°C), 1–2 hours, and then refrigerate overnight, 8–10 hours.

recipe continues

FINAL DOUGH (DAY 2, MORNING)

INGREDIENT	GRAMS	OUNCES	VOLUME
Scald	867	30.60	Use all
Coarse rye meal	240	8.50	1½ cups
Medium rye flour	240	8.50	1⅞ cups
Cracked wheat	240	8.50	1⅔ cups
Warm (105°F/41°C) water	400	14.10	1⅔ cups
Instant yeast	20	0.70	5 tsp.
Light molasses or malt syrup	240	8.50	¾ cup
Vegetable shortening for pan	As needed		

2. Combine the scald and the remaining ingredients in the mixer and use the flat paddle at low (KA2) speed to mix until the dough develops into a dense, viscous mass, 12–15 minutes. Use a plastic dough scraper and wet hands to transfer the dough to a well-greased 9-by-4-by-4-inch/23-by-10-by-10 cm Pullman loaf pan or 9-by-5-by-3-inch/23-by-13-by-8 cm standard loaf pan, cover, and proof at room temperature for 40–45 minutes. There will be little or no visible expansion of the dough.

3. Preheat the oven to 465°F/240° C with a steam pan (see page 76) and the baking surface in the middle. Use a chopstick, skewer, or docking wheel to dock the loaf thoroughly to a depth of ¼–½ inch/0.6–1.25 cm. Lower the oven temperature to 410°F/210°C and bake with steam for 10 minutes, then remove the steam pan and bake for another 35 minutes. Lower the temperature to 350°F/175°C and bake until the loaf thumps when tapped with a finger and the internal temperature is at least 198°F/92°C, another 30–40 minutes. Remove from the pan and transfer to a rack and cool thoroughly. For best flavor, let the bread rest for 24–48 hours before slicing.

BAKER'S PERCENTAGES

INGREDIENT	G	%
TOTAL FLOUR	960	100.00%
Medium rye flour	480	50.00%
Coarse rye meal	240	25.00%
Cracked wheat	240	25.00%
Water	800	83.33%
Salt	27	2.78%
Instant yeast	20	2.08%
Syrup	240	25.00%
Sunflower seeds	160	16.67%
Flaxseed	40	4.17%
TOTAL FORMULA	2,247	234.03%

For a pumpkinseed lover like me, **Pumpkinseed Rye** is heavenly, loaded as it is with crunchy flaxseed and sweet, rich pumpkinseeds in a rustic sour-bitter crumb.

Pumpkinseed Rye

Kürbiskernbrot

GERMANY   When I was a kid in Brooklyn, the candy stores used to sell little boxes of heavily salted roasted pumpkinseeds that we cracked with our teeth. Once we got past the salt, we were rewarded with sweet green kernels whose abundant fat content soothed our brined tongues. The salt was the price we paid for the pleasure of the seeds.

This is a bread that appeals to my love of pumpkinseeds—and one that more Americans ought to know about. Texturally it's amazing—a medley of pumpkinseeds, crunchy flaxseed, and chewy coarse rye meal, all encased in a tender wheat-rye crumb. The pumpkinseeds dominate its flavor profile, their sweet richness accented by the burnt notes of black rye malt and moderately sour finish. Serve this bread with pork schnitzel or a bowl of butternut squash soup, accompanied by a glass of chilled riesling.

RYE %:	69%
STAGES:	Sponge, soaker, final dough
LEAVEN:	Rye sour culture, yeast
START TO FINISH:	13–16 hours
HANDS-ON TIME:	30–40 minutes
YIELD:	One 2 lb./900 g loaf

SPONGE (DAY 1, EVENING)

INGREDIENT	GRAMS	OUNCES	VOLUME	BAKER'S PERCENTAGE
Medium rye flour	123	4.35	1 cup	100%
Warm (105°F/41°C) water	123	4.35	½ cup	100%
Rye sour culture (see page 35)	12	0.40	1 Tbs.	10%

recipe continues

1. Mix the sponge ingredients by hand until incorporated, cover, and ferment at room temperature (68–72°F/20–22°C) overnight, 10–12 hours. The sponge will be very bubbly, have a clean sour smell, and will have doubled in volume.

SOAKER (DAY 1, EVENING)

INGREDIENT	GRAMS	OUNCES	VOLUME	BAKER'S PERCENTAGE
Pumpkinseeds	150	5.30	1¼ cups	100%
Warm (105°F/41°C) water	125	4.40	½ cup	83%
Flaxseed	30	1.05	3 Tbs.	20%
Coarse rye meal	20	0.70	2 Tbs.	13%
AP flour	20	0.70	2¼ Tbs.	13%
Salt	9	0.30	1½ tsp.	6%
Black rye malt (see page 42)	8	0.30	1 tsp.	5%

2. Mix the soaker ingredients by hand until blended, cover, and let stand at room temperature overnight, 10–12 hours.

FINAL DOUGH (DAY 2, MORNING)

INGREDIENT	GRAMS	OUNCES	VOLUME
Soaker	362	12.75	Use all
Sponge	258	9.10	Use all
Medium rye flour	167	5.85	1⅓ cups
Bread flour	120	4.25	¾–1 cup
Warm (105°F/41°C) water	172	6.05	¾ cup
Instant yeast	2	0.05	⅓ tsp.
Flour for dusting	As needed		

3. Combine the soaker, sponge, flours, warm water, and yeast in the mixer. Use the dough hook at low (KA2) speed to mix, scraping down the bowl as necessary, until a stiff dough forms, 10–12 minutes. Cover and ferment at room temperature until barely expanded, 20–30 minutes.

4. Turn the dough onto a well-floured work surface and shape into a ball, then place seam side up in a well-floured round or oval bread form (see page 72) or cloth-lined proofing basket. Cover and proof at room temperature until the loaf has visibly expanded and shows cracks or broken bubbles, 60–75 minutes.

5. Preheat the oven to 485°F/250°C with a steam pan (see page 76) and the baking surface in the middle. Turn the loaf seam side down onto a floured peel, if using a baking stone, or parchment-lined sheet pan, slash to a depth of ¼–½ inch/0.6–1.25 cm, and brush the top crust generously with water. Bake with steam for 5 minutes, then remove the steam pan, lower the temperature to 390°F/200°C, and continue baking until the loaf thumps when tapped with a finger and the internal temperature is at least 198°F/92°C, 45–50 minutes. Transfer to a rack and cool thoroughly before slicing.

BAKER'S PERCENTAGES

INGREDIENT	G	%
TOTAL FLOUR	450	100.00%
Medium rye flour	290	64.42%
Bread flour	140	31.14%
Coarse rye meal	20	4.44%
Water	295	65.55%
Salt	9	2.00%
Instant yeast	2	0.44%
Pumpkinseeds	150	33.33%
Soaker water	125	27.77%
Flaxseed	30	6.66%
Black rye malt	8	1.78%
Rye sour culture	12	2.67%
TOTAL FORMULA	1,081	240.11%
Total flour prefermented	123	27.32%

Frisian Black Bread

Fries Swartbrood

HOLLAND This is a very simple bread — just fine rye meal, bread flour, water, salt, and rye sour culture—but one that's enormously tasty, with a moist, tender crumb, a chewy crust, and a mouth-awakening sour edge. The bread is unusual because it starts with a very loose, extremely vigorous two-stage sponge that's more like a batter. The sponge provides a strong boost of acidity and leavening power to the finished dough, so there's very little "starch attack" (see page 32) even though the baking starts in a cold oven. Try this bread with a topping like an aged Gouda or with peanut butter and jelly.

RYE %:	50%
STAGES:	**2-stage sponge, final dough**
LEAVEN:	**Rye sour culture**
START TO FINISH:	**18–22 hours**
HANDS-ON TIME:	**30–40 minutes**
YIELD:	**One 2¾ lb./1.20 kg loaf**

STAGE 1 SPONGE (DAY 1, EVENING)

INGREDIENT	GRAMS	OUNCES	VOLUME	BAKER'S PERCENTAGE
Fine rye meal or medium rye flour	167	5.90	¾–1 cup	100%
Water	333	11.75	1½ cups less 1 tsp.	200%
Rye sour culture (see page 35)	20	0.70	1½ Tbs.	12%

1. Mix the Stage 1 sponge ingredients by hand until incorporated, cover, and ferment at room temperature (68–72°F/20–22°C) overnight, 10–12 hours. The sponge will be very bubbly, have a clean sour smell, and will have doubled in volume.

STAGE 2 SPONGE (DAY 2, MORNING)

INGREDIENT	GRAMS	OUNCES	VOLUME	BAKER'S PERCENTAGE
Fine rye meal or medium rye flour	167	5.90	¾–1 cup	50%
Bread flour	167	5.90	1¼–1½ cups	50%
Water	250	8.80	1 cup + 2 Tbs.	75%
Stage 1 sponge	520	18.35	Use all	156%

2. Add the rye meal, bread flour, and water to the sponge, mix by hand to incorporate, cover, and ferment at room temperature until bubbly and well expanded, 6–8 hours.

FINAL DOUGH (DAY 2, AFTERNOON)

INGREDIENT	GRAMS	OUNCES	VOLUME
Stage 2 sponge	1,104	38.95	Use all
Bread flour	167	5.90	1⅜ cups
Salt	12	0.40	2 tsp.
Honey	28	1.00	4 tsp.
Vegetable shortening for pan	As needed		

3. Combine the sponge, flour, salt, and honey in the mixer and use the paddle at low (KA2) speed to mix until the dough is thick but still fluid, like a heavy batter, 6–8 minutes. Cover and ferment at room temperature until the surface of the dough shows bubbles, 30–45 minutes.

4. Pour the dough into a well-greased 9-by-4-by-4-inch/23-by-10-by-10 cm Pullman loaf pan or standard 9-by-5-inch/23-by-13 cm loaf pan, put it into a cold oven, and proof until the dough approaches the rim of the pan, 30–45 minutes.

5. Heat the oven to 460°F/240°C with the baking surface in the middle. Once the oven has reached temperature, bake for 20 minutes, then lower the temperature 375°F/190°C and continue baking until the loaf thumps when tapped with a finger and the internal temperature is at least 198°F/92°C, 75–80 minutes. Remove from the pan and transfer to a rack. Let stand at least 24 hours before slicing.

recipe continues

BAKER'S PERCENTAGES

INGREDIENT	G	%
TOTAL FLOUR	666	100.00%
Rye flour	333	50.00%
Bread flour	333	50.00%
Water	583	87.50%
Salt	12	1.80%
Honey	28	4.25%
Rye sour culture	20	3.00%
TOTAL FORMULA	1,309	196.55%
Total flour prefermented	500	75.00%

Scorched-Crust Sour Rye

Gersterbrot

GERMANY Of all the rye breads I've encountered, this one stands out for its charred and blistered top crust. The scorching comes from the traditional practice of baking the loaves at high heat, packed tightly together inside wood-fired ovens. This gave them a rectangular cross section, kept the side crusts soft, and caused the top crust to bubble and char.

Since I don't have a wood-fired oven—and, even if I did, probably wouldn't make enough loaves to pack it wall-to-wall—I do what German home bakers do when they make this bread: use a blowtorch. Applied just before the panned bread goes into the oven, the torch cooks the top crust, creating a hard skin and raising bubbles that blacken in the heat. Beneath that hard, speckled crust is a firm, chewy crumb and pleasing sweet-sour balance, with a touch of bitterness from the char. It's a fine all-around sandwich bread, as suitable for ham and cheese or a turkey club as it is for cream cheese and jelly.

RYE %:	**79%**
STAGES:	**Sponge, final dough**
LEAVEN:	**Rye sour culture, yeast**
START TO FINISH:	**10–12 hours**
HANDS-ON TIME:	**30–45 minutes**
YIELD:	**One 2½ lb./1.15 kg loaf**

SPONGE (DAY 1, EVENING)

INGREDIENT	GRAMS	OUNCES	VOLUME	BAKER'S PERCENTAGE
Medium rye flour	265	9.35	2 cups	100%
Warm (105°F/41°C) water	265	9.35	1⅛ cups	100%
Rye sour culture (see page 35)	27	0.95	3 Tbs.	10%

1. Mix the sponge ingredients by hand until incorporated, cover, and ferment at room temperature (68–72°F/20–22°C) overnight, 10–12 hours. The sponge will be very bubbly, have a clean sour smell, and will have doubled in volume.

recipe continues

Scorched-Crust Sour Rye is a traditional North German bread that features a firm, chewy crumb and a nice balance of sweet and sour. Instead of using the high heat of a wood-fired oven, scorch the top crust with a blowtorch.

FINAL DOUGH (DAY 2, MORNING)

INGREDIENT	GRAMS	OUNCES	VOLUME
Sponge	557	19.65	Use all
White rye flour	175	6.15	1¼ cups
First clear or high-gluten flour	140	4.95	1 cup
Medium rye flour	100	3.55	¾ cup
Warm (105°F/41°C) water	180	6.35	¾ cup
Salt	14	0.50	2¼ tsp.
Instant yeast	4	0.15	1 tsp.
Flour for dusting	As needed		
Vegetable shortening for pan	As needed		

2. Combine the sponge, flours, warm water, salt, and yeast in the mixer and use the dough hook at low (KA2) speed to mix until the dough pulls away from the sides of the bowl and comes together in a ball, 7–8 minutes. Cover and ferment at room temperature until the dough has visibly expanded, 30–45 minutes.

3. Turn the dough onto a lightly floured work surface, knead briefly, and form it into an oblong loaf. Place the loaf, seam side down, in a well-greased 9-by-4-by-4-inch/23-by-10-by-10 cm Pullman loaf pan or 9-by-5-inch/23-by-13 cm loaf pan. Cover and proof at room temperature until the dough reaches the rim of the pan, 60–75 minutes. Use a blowtorch (available at hardware stores) to scorch the top crust until it blisters and small black flecks appear, 3–5 minutes.

4. Preheat the oven to 500°F/260°C with a steam pan (see page 76) and the baking surface in the middle. Bake with steam for 15 minutes, then remove the steam pan, lower the oven temperature to 400°F/200°C, and bake 35–40 minutes more. Remove the loaf from the pan, reduce the temperature to 350°F/180°C, and return the bread to the oven. Bake until the loaf thumps when tapped with a finger and the internal temperature is at least 198°F/92°C, 10–15 minutes. Transfer to a rack and cool thoroughly before slicing.

recipe continues

BAKER'S PERCENTAGES

INGREDIENT	G	%
TOTAL FLOUR	680	100.00%
Medium rye flour	365	53.67%
White rye flour	175	25.74%
First clear flour	140	20.59%
Water	445	65.44%
Salt	14	2.06%
Instant yeast	4	0.59%
Rye sour culture	27	3.97%
TOTAL FORMULA	1,170	172.06%
Total flour prefermented	265	38.97%

Salty Rye Rolls

Sigteboller

DENMARK In baking my way through a wide variety of northern rye breads, I came to expect a crumb that was dense and chewy. Imagine my surprise and pleasure when I baked these rolls, which delight on many levels. In taste and texture they are a study in contrasts—the sting and astringent edge of salt and caraway topping against the sweet earthiness of rye and molasses; the crunch of the topping against the delicacy of the crumb. These are wonderful all-around rolls, equally tasty with cream cheese, jam, or butter at breakfast or as a slider bun or dinner roll. I like them a lot.

RYE %:	56%
STAGES:	**Straight dough**
LEAVEN:	**Yeast**
START TO FINISH:	**2½–3 hours**
HANDS-ON TIME:	**30–40 minutes**
YIELD:	**One dozen 2½ oz./70 g rolls**

DOUGH

INGREDIENT	GRAMS	OUNCES	VOLUME	BAKER'S PERCENTAGE
Medium rye flour	314	11.10	2½ cups	55.67%
Bread flour	250	8.80	1¾ cups	44.33%
Instant yeast	10	0.35	1 Tbs.	1.77%
Salt	7	0.25	1 tsp.	1.24%
Unsulphured dark molasses	23	0.80	1 Tbs.	4.08%
Warm (105°F/41°C) water	350	12.35	1½ cups	62.06%
TOTAL FORMULA	954	10.20		169.15%
Total flour	564	19.90		100.00%
Bread flour for dusting	As needed			

recipe continues

1. Combine the flours, yeast, and salt in the mixer. Dissolve the molasses in the water, then add to the dry ingredients and use the dough hook at low (KA2) speed until the dough leaves the sides of the bowl and forms a smooth, elastic mass, 6–8 minutes. Cover and ferment at room temperature (68–72°F/20–22°C) until doubled, about 1 hour.

2. Turn the dough, which will be soft, pliable, and tacky, onto a lightly floured surface. Knead gently back to its original volume and divide into twelve pieces weighing about 80 g/2¾ oz. each.

TOPPING

INGREDIENT	GRAMS	OUNCES	VOLUME
Rolled oats	56	2.00	¾ cup
Caraway seed	7	0.25	1 Tbs.
Kosher salt	14	0.50	1 Tbs.

3. Roll each dough piece into a ball, press the bottom (seam side) into the rolled oats, then place on a parchment-lined sheet pan. Cover and proof at room temperature until the dough has expanded to twice its original size, 40–50 minutes.

4. Preheat the oven to 375°F/190°C with the baking surface in the upper third. Slash the rolls once to a depth of ¼–½ inch/0.6–1.25 cm, brush generously with water, and sprinkle with caraway first and then salt. Bake until the crust is light to medium brown, 20–25 minutes. Let cool on the pan.

Salty Rye Rolls are a study in contrasts: the sweetness of rye and the astringent sting of salt and caraway; a close, tender crumb against the crunch of crust and topping.

A relic of the Cold War, **East Berlin Malt Rye** pairs the burnt coffee, chocolate, and caramel notes of dark-roasted barley malt with a clean sour finish reminiscent of the best sour beers.

East Berlin Malt Rye

Malfabrot

GERMANY *Malfabrot* was first introduced in late 1940s by the East Berlin State-Owned Baked Goods Collective (*VEB Backwarenkombinat*),[62] making it a genuine relic of the Cold War. Its name is a shortened form of the German word for malt factory, *Malzfabrik*, a reference to its 10% roasted barley malt content. With its strong flavor and dense crumb, *Malfabrot* gained a wide following and quickly became East Germany's signature bread. It's still produced today.

If you love craft sour beers, you'll love this tender, close-crumbed bread. The malt is incredibly fragrant and sweet, with strong chocolate, caramel, and coffee notes from the roasting. The sponge, which constitutes nearly half of the total dough, adds an assertive sour edge. All in all, a tasty and unusual bread. So no matter what other negatives came out of the former East Germany—think Trabant, arguably the worst car ever built—this is one contribution that's 100% positive.

RYE %:	**75%**
STAGES:	**Sponge, final dough**
LEAVEN:	**Rye sour culture, yeast**
START TO FINISH:	**13–15 hours**
HANDS-ON TIME:	**30–40 minutes**
YIELD:	**Two 1¾ lb./800 g loaves**

SPONGE (DAY 1, EVENING)

INGREDIENT	GRAMS	OUNCES	VOLUME	BAKER'S PERCENTAGE
Medium rye flour	375	13.25	1⅔ cups	100%
Warm (105°F/41°C) water	375	13.25	1 cup	100%
Rye sour culture (see page 35)	38	1.35	2½ Tbs.	10%

1. Mix the sponge ingredients by hand until incorporated, cover, and ferment at room temperature (68–72°F/20–22°C) overnight, 10–12 hours. The sponge will be very bubbly, have a clean sour smell, and will have doubled in volume.

recipe continues

FINAL DOUGH (DAY 2, MORNING)

INGREDIENT	GRAMS	OUNCES	VOLUME
Sponge	788	27.85	Use all
White rye flour	250	8.80	1¾ cups
Medium rye flour	125	4.40	1 cup
AP flour	150	5.30	1 cup + 3 Tbs.
Malted barley flour (see Note)	100	3.55	⅔ cup
Warm (105°F/41°C) water	300	10.60	1¼ cups
Salt	18	0.65	1 Tbs.
Instant yeast	4	0.15	1 tsp.
Flour for dusting	As needed		

2. Combine the sponge, flours, malted barley flour, warm water, salt, and yeast in the mixer and use the dough hook at low (KA2) speed to mix until the dough is evenly colored and climbs up the hook, 6–8 minutes. Cover and ferment at room temperature until the dough visibly expands, 45–60 minutes.

3. Turn the dough, which will be very soft and sticky but cohesive, onto a well-floured work surface, use floured hands to knead back to its original volume, and divide it into two pieces, each weighing about 825 g/29 oz. Shape each into a boule or an oblong and place, seam side up, in a well-floured round or oval bread form (see page 72) or cloth-lined basket. Cover and proof at room temperature until the surface of the dough shows cracking, 45–60 minutes.

4. Preheat the oven to 480°F/240°C with a steam pan (see page 76) and the baking surface in the middle. Turn the loaves onto a well-floured peel, if using a baking stone, or onto a parchment-lined sheet pan. Bake with steam for 15 minutes, then remove the steam pan, lower the oven temperature to 430°F/220°C, and bake until the loaf thumps when tapped with a finger and the internal temperature is at least 198°F/92°C, 30–35 minutes. Transfer to a rack and cool thoroughly before slicing.

Note: Malted barley is generally available at local home brew supply stores and through online vendors. I use crystal malt 120L, which is a fairly dark roast, with pronounced chocolate-coffee notes, but lighter roasts are also available if you prefer a less intense flavor profile. Put the malt through a grain mill or use a blender or food processor to pulse it to a powder, then sift out the husks and germ. Alternatively, get some regular barley flour and roast it carefully in a skillet over medium heat, stirring constantly to prevent scorching, until it turns nut brown.

BAKER'S PERCENTAGES

INGREDIENT	G	%
TOTAL FLOUR	1,000	100.00%
Medium rye flour	500	50.00%
White rye flour	250	25.00%
AP flour	150	15.00%
Malted barley	100	10.00%
Water	675	67.50%
Salt	18	1.80%
Instant yeast	4	0.40%
Rye sour culture	38	3.80%
TOTAL FORMULA	1,735	173.50%
Total flour prefermented	375	37.50%

BAKER'S PERCENTAGES

INGREDIENT	G	%
Medium rye flour	300	100.00%
Water	50	16.67%
Malt or corn syrup	150	50.00%
Molasses	100	33.33%
Candied citrus peel	80	26.67%
Brown sugar	75	25.00%
Candied ginger	40	13.33%
Baking soda	3	1.00%
Baking powder	5	1.67%
Spices	10	3.17%
TOTAL FORMULA	813	270.83%

Ammerland Black Bread

Ammerländer Schwarzbrot

GERMANY   This bread fooled me. When I first baked it, I was expecting an intensely flavored, very sour bread consistent with its North German provenance. Instead, I got a firm, chewy, subtly flavored bread that showcases both the texture and sweetness of coarsely milled rye and wheat against a mild and clean sour finish. This is a very dense loaf: 4 pounds of dough, nearly 2 kilograms, in a single loaf. That's a lot of bread, but it will stay fresh for weeks and freezes nicely.

This is a bread that demands discovery. My first bite was something of a letdown, since I expected stronger flavors. By the third bite, though, I was hooked. One slice followed another, first by itself, then with a film of butter, followed by a medium Ammerland-style Swiss cheese, smoked salmon, and finally with a very ripe *triple-crème* Délice de Bourgogne. As I slowly chewed each pairing, savoring and deconstructing the contrasting flavors and textures, the Ammerländer seduced me completely.

RYE %:	**80%**
STAGES:	**Sponge, final dough**
LEAVEN:	**Rye sour culture**
START TO FINISH:	**16–18 hours**
HANDS-ON TIME:	**30–40 minutes**
YIELD:	**One 4 lb./1.8 kg loaf**

SPONGE (DAY 1, EVENING)

INGREDIENT	GRAMS	OUNCES	VOLUME	BAKER'S PERCENTAGE
Coarse rye meal	480	16.95	3 cups	80%
Cracked wheat	120	4.25	¾ cup	20%
Warm (105°F/41°C) water	600	21.15	2½ cups	100%
Rye sour culture (see page 35)	55	1.95	¼ cup	9%

recipe continues

SCALD (DAY 1, AFTERNOON)

INGREDIENT	GRAMS	OUNCES	VOLUME	BAKER'S PERCENTAGE
Coarse rye meal	240	8.45	1½ cups	100%
Boiling water	192	6.75	¾ cup + 2 Tbs.	80%
Salt	18	0.60	1 Tbs.	7%

2. Combine the scald ingredients, cover, and let stand at room temperature for 16–18 hours.

SOAKER (DAY 1, AFTERNOON)

INGREDIENT	GRAMS	OUNCES	VOLUME	BAKER'S PERCENTAGE
Sunflower seeds	160	5.65	1⅛ cups	100%
Warm (105°F/41°C) water	320	11.30	1⅓ cups	200%
Flaxseed	80	2.80	½ cup	50%
Stale rye bread, crumbled	80	2.80	¾ cup	50%

3. In a separate bowl, combine the soaker ingredients, stir to blend, cover, and let stand for 16–18 hours.

FINAL DOUGH (DAY 2, MORNING)

INGREDIENT	GRAMS	OUNCES	VOLUME
Sponge	485	17.10	Use all
Scald	450	15.80	Use all
Soaker	640	22.55	Use all
Coarse rye meal	250	8.80	2 cups
Medium rye flour	70	2.50	⅝ cup
Warm (105°F/41°C) water	128	4.50	½ cup + 1 Tbs.
Instant yeast	2	0.05	½ tsp.
Malt syrup, light molasses, honey, or beet syrup	40	1.40	⅛ cup
Vegetable shortening for pan	As needed		
Sunflower seeds for topping	As needed		

4. Combine the sponge, scald, and soaker with the rye meal and flour, warm water, yeast, and syrup in the mixer and use the paddle at low (KA2) speed to mix until the dough comes together in a dense, sticky mass and the rye meal kernels have broken up, 30–35 minutes. Cover and ferment at room temperature until visibly expanded, 45–60 minutes.

5. Return the dough to the mixer and use the dough hook at low (KA2) speed, scraping down the bowl as necessary, until the dough is back to its original volume, 5–6 minutes. Then use a plastic dough scraper and wet hands to transfer it into a well-greased 9-by-4-by-4-inch/23-by-10-by-10 cm Pullman loaf pan or 9-by-5-by-3-inch/23-by-13-by-8 cm loaf pan. Smooth the top with wet hands, then cover and proof at room temperature until the dough has risen about 1 inch/2.5 cm, 30–40 minutes.

6. Preheat the oven to 465°F/240°C with a steam pan (see page 76) and the baking surface in the middle. Use a docking wheel, chopstick, or skewer to dock the loaf thoroughly to a depth of at least ½ inch/1.25 cm, brush with water, and sprinkle liberally with sunflower seed. Bake with steam for 5 minutes, then remove the steam pan. Bake for 15 minutes more at 465°F/240°C, then lower the temperature to 390°F/200°C and bake until the loaf thumps when tapped with a finger and the internal temperature is at least 198°F/92°C, about 90 minutes. Transfer to a rack and let stand for 24–48 hours before slicing.

recipe continues

FINAL DOUGH (DAY 2, MORNING)

INGREDIENT	GRAMS	OUNCES	VOLUME
Sponge	635	22.4	Use all
White rye flour	350	12.35	2½ cups
Light beer, such as Pilsner, lager, or *hefeweizen*	210	7.40	1 cup less 1 Tbs.
Salt	14	0.50	2¼ tsp.
Instant yeast	4	0.15	1 tsp.
Malt syrup, unsulphured dark molasses, or dark corn syrup	14	0.50	1¾ tsp.
Caraway seed	2	0.07	1 tsp.
White rye flour for dusting	As needed		
Caraway seed for topping	5	0.15	2 tsp.
Kosher salt for topping	7	0.25	1–1½ tsp.

2. Combine the sponge, flour, beer, salt, yeast, malt syrup, and caraway seed in the mixer. Use the dough hook at low (KA2) speed until fully developed, 7–8 minutes, then cover and ferment at room temperature (68–72°F/20–22°C) until nearly doubled in bulk, 30–45 minutes.

3. Turn the dough onto a well-floured work surface, knead it back to its original volume, and divide into a dozen 100 g/3½ oz. pieces. Gently roll each piece into a slightly flattened ball and place about 1 inch/2.5 cm apart on a parchment-lined baking sheet. Cover and proof at room temperature until cracks or broken bubbles appear on the surface of the dough, 30–40 minutes.

4. Preheat the oven to 465°F/240°C with a steam pan (see page 76) and the baking surface in the middle. Use a sharp knife or razor blade to score the rolls in a diamond pattern to a depth of ¼–½ inch/0.6–1.25 cm, brush with water, and sprinkle with caraway seed and then kosher salt. Bake with steam for 10 minutes, remove the steam pan, and continue baking until golden brown, 10–12 minutes longer. Transfer to a rack and cool thoroughly.

BAKER'S PERCENTAGES

INGREDIENT	G	%
TOTAL FLOUR	680	100.00%
White rye flour	350	51.47%
Medium rye flour	330	48.53%
Water	270	39.71%
Beer	210	30.88%
Salt	14	2.06%
Instant yeast	6	0.88%
Malt syrup	14	2.06%
Rye sour culture	33	4.85%
TOTAL FORMULA	1,227	180.44%
Total flour prefermented	330	48.53%

Sweet and Crisp: Sweden, Finland, and Iceland

RYE has been cultivated in Sweden and Finland for more than fifteen hundred years and has shaped their cultures. In the boreal forests of the subarctic North, where water powered the mills, baking took place twice a year, after the spring and autumn floods. The breads were austere, sour, and had to last for months. They had a hole in the center for storing on poles hung from the ceiling and became so hard that it sometimes took a wood plane to cut them.[63] The Finns even had their own rye god, Rukiin Jumala, whose favor produced bountiful harvests.

To the south, on the sandy coastal plains along the Baltic Sea and the Gulfs of Bothnia and Finland, life was easier. The Humboldt current warmed the climate.

Wind powered the mills, so that baking was a more frequent occurrence. The breads were hydrated with milk and beer, sweetened with syrup, and perfumed with spices brought in by Hanseatic traders.

The regional distinctions continue to this day. The breads of southern Sweden and Finland—"Archipelago" Bread (page 166), Sweet Limpa (page 185) and Helsinki Buttermilk Rye (page 172)—are soft, sweet, aromatic, and leavened with yeast or baking soda. The breads of the North—Honey-Flaxseed Crispbread (page 169), Sour Ring Bread (page 181), and Slow-Baked Finnish Rye (page 190)—are hard, sour, and austere. Taken in totality, they represent the history and traditions of an entire region.

"Archipelago" Bread

Skärgårdslimpa

SWEDEN The Stockholm Archipelago is a collection of more than 30,000 islands, skerries, and rocks that extends from Stockholm roughly 60 kilometers (37 miles) to the east. My friend and mentor, John Kanni, who spent many years baking professionally in Sweden, loves this Stockholm bread, and so do I. It's a quick bread, leavened with baking soda and buttermilk, and it's loaded with texture and flavor. The crumb is dense, dominated by the rustic mouthfeel of coarse rye meal and cracked wheat, and punctuated with juicy raisins and the crunch of flax and sunflower seeds. The flavor profile is a complex of sweet, acid, and nutty, with delicate burnt sugar notes from the molasses. This is a bread that, topped with cream cheese, Brie, or roast beef or just plain, goes beautifully with a cup of coffee.

RYE %:	**21%**
STAGES:	**Straight dough**
LEAVEN:	**Baking soda**
START TO FINISH:	**2 hours**
HANDS-ON TIME:	**15–20 minutes**
YIELD:	**Two 2¼ lb./1 kg loaves**

DOUGH

INGREDIENT	GRAMS	OUNCES	VOLUME	BAKER'S PERCENTAGE
Bread flour	432	15.25	3⅛ cups	51.74%
Coarse rye meal	173	6.10	1⅛ cups	20.72%
Cracked wheat	124	4.35	⅞ cup	14.85%
Wheat bran	106	3.70	1¾ cups	12.69%
Buttermilk	720	25.40	3 cups	86.23%
Salt	5	0.15	¾ tsp.	0.60%
Honey	150	5.30	½ cup	17.96%
Unsulphured dark molasses	150	5.30	½ cup	17.96%

Raisins	144	5.10	⅞ cup	17.25%
Flaxseed	101	3.55	⅝ cup	12.10%
Sunflower seeds	82	2.90	⅝ cup	9.82%
Baking soda	17	0.60	4 tsp.	2.04%
TOTAL FORMULA	2,204	77.70		263.95%
Vegetable shortening for pans	As needed			

1. Combine all of the dough ingredients and mix until evenly blended into a thick batter, 8–10 minutes by hand or, using the paddle at low (KA2) speed, 5–6 minutes by machine. Pour into two well-greased 8½-by-4½-by-2¾-inch/22-by-12-by-7 cm loaf pans and use a wet spatula or dough scraper to mound the center of each loaf.

2. Preheat the oven to 300°F/150°C with the baking surface in the middle. Bake until the top crust is deeply browned and the internal temperature is at least 198°F/92°C, 1½–2 hours. Transfer from pans to a rack and cool thoroughly before slicing.

Honey-Flaxseed Crispbread. In Scandinavia's far north, baking only took place twice a year, so the rye bakers made their breads crisp and round, with a hole in the middle so they could be stored on poles hung from the ceiling.

Honey-Flaxseed Crispbread

Rågsurdegen Knäckebröd

SWEDEN Until I baked this one, my experience of Scandinavian crispbread was limited to the oblong sheets of rye cracker that come in paper-wrapped bricks. These crunchy circular flatbreads hark back to the traditions of northern Scandinavia, where yeast barely survives and baking took place only twice a year. Like other Nordic breads, these have a hole in the center so they can be stored on poles suspended from the ceiling over the long subarctic winters.

This is a hearty, richly flavored bread that can last for months. Its dominant flavor is rye with a light sour edge. Its texture is pure crunch, complemented by the crackle of flaxseed and the sweet richness of sesame. Substitute these, broken up, wherever you use other kinds of crackers—with cheeses, dips, and charcuterie; you'll never go back to store-bought again.

RYE %:	**75%**
STAGES:	**2-stage sponge, final dough**
LEAVEN:	**Rye sour culture, yeast**
START TO FINISH:	**10–14 hours**
HANDS-ON TIME:	**45–60 minutes**
YIELD:	**One dozen 4 oz./115 g breads**

STAGE 1 SPONGE (DAY 1, EVENING)

INGREDIENT	GRAMS	OUNCES	VOLUME	BAKER'S PERCENTAGE
Medium rye flour	47	1.67	⅓ cup	100%
Warm (105°F/41°C) water	47	1.68	¼ cup less 1 tsp.	100%
Rye sour culture (see page 35)	6	0.20	1¼ tsp.	13%

1. Mix the sponge ingredients by hand until incorporated, cover, and ferment at room temperature (68–72°F/20–22°C) overnight, 10–12 hours. The sponge will be very bubbly, have a clean sour smell, and will have doubled in volume.

recipe continues

Rye Biscuits

Rågkex

SWEDEN These flaky biscuits are about as quick and easy a rye recipe as you're likely to find. Their sweet, buttery flavor and chewy texture have made them a favorite at our weekend brunches. For an extra fillip of fragrance and bite, add a teaspoon or two of caraway seeds. This is a chew that's so distinctive and versatile that it goes equally well with homemade preserves, scrambled eggs, and stinky-ripe cheeses.

RYE %:	**100%**
STAGES:	**Straight dough**
LEAVEN:	**Baking powder**
START TO FINISH:	**40 minutes**
HANDS-ON TIME:	**20–25 minutes**
YIELD:	**About 2 dozen 3-inch/8 cm biscuits**

DOUGH

INGREDIENT	GRAMS	OUNCES	VOLUME	BAKER'S PERCENTAGE
Medium rye meal	250	8.80	1⅔ cups	50.00%
Medium rye flour	250	8.80	2 cups	50.00%
Whole milk	300	10.60	1¼ cups	60.00%
Salt	6	0.20	1 tsp.	1.20%
Baking powder	9	0.30	2 tsp.	1.80%
Sugar	4	0.15	1 tsp.	0.80%
Unsalted butter, at room temperature (68–72°F/20–22°C)	114	4.00	½ cup	22.80%
Caraway, anise, fennel, or dill seed (optional)	6	0.20	2½ tsp.	1.20%
TOTAL FORMULA	939	33.05		187.80%
Flour for dusting	As needed			
Total flour	500	17.60		100.00%

1. Combine the dough ingredients, adding the butter in teaspoon-sized pieces, and mix by hand into a fairly stiff dough.

2. Turn onto a well-floured work surface and roll ¼-inch/0.6 cm thick, then use a biscuit cutter or drinking glass to cut rounds or use a pizza wheel or sharp knife to cut into squares. Reroll any excess dough and continue cutting until it's all used up.

3. Preheat the oven to 390°F/200°C with the baking surface in the upper third. Arrange the biscuits 1 inch/2.5 cm apart on parchment-lined baking sheets, dock thoroughly with a fork or chopstick to a depth of ¼–½ inch/0.6–1.25 cm, and bake until risen and golden brown, 12–15 minutes. Eat warm with butter, honey, or jam.

plastic wrap, and proof at room temperature until the dough has clearly risen and broken bubbles appear on the surface of the dough, 30–45 minutes.

5. Preheat the oven to 435°F/225°C with the baking surface in the lower third. Brush each loaf with water and bake for 15 minutes. Reduce the heat to 390°F/200°C and continue baking until the internal temperature is at least 198°F/92°C, about 40 minutes. Remove from the pan, transfer to a rack, and brush with boiling water. Cool thoroughly before slicing.

BAKER'S PERCENTAGES

INGREDIENT	G	%
TOTAL FLOUR	600	100.00%
Medium rye flour	300	50.00%
Bread flour	300	50.00%
Water	553	92.08%
Salt	9	1.50%
Instant yeast	10	1.67%
Syrup	115	19.17%
Vinegar	7	1.17%
Dried orange peel	7	1.17%
TOTAL FORMULA	1,301	216.76%

Rye Tortillas

Flatbrauð

ICELAND Soft griddle-baked flatbreads are a staple food in the Nordic countries and among Scandinavian communities abroad. When I was in graduate school at the University of Wisconsin, it was common for the local Norwegian churches to sponsor dinners that featured the gelatinous lye-treated dried cod called *lutefisk* and *lefse*, a potato-wheat flatbread. In Sweden and the Upper Midwest, griddle-baked wheat, barley, or rye "thin breads" (*tunnbröd*) abound. In Iceland these 100% rye flatbreads are the favorite.

It was a food emergency that prompted me to make this bread for the first time. I was making fish tacos—a Southern California favorite—for dinner, only to discover while the fish was frying that the tortillas I knew for certain we had in our pantry were nowhere to be found. I'd been thinking about making *flatbrauð* for some time, and this was the perfect opportunity.

It was a great experience. The breads were fast, easy, and flavorful: their nutty sweetness—like a corn tortilla with the smoothness of a flour tortillas—made them a perfect foil for the fish, shredded cabbage, and mayonnaise-salsa dressing. I stored the leftover flatbreads in a plastic bag and toasted them on a griddle the next morning for breakfast. Spread with butter and apricot jam, they were heavenly. Since that day, they've become a regular in my home.

RYE %:	**100%**
STAGES:	**Straight dough**
LEAVEN:	**None**
START TO FINISH:	**30–40 minutes**
HANDS-ON TIME:	**30–40 minutes**
YIELD:	**One dozen 3 oz./85 g breads**

recipe continues

DOUGH

INGREDIENT	GRAMS	OUNCES	VOLUME	BAKER'S PERCENTAGE
Medium rye flour	665	23.45	5¼ cups	100.00%
Warm (105°F/41°C) water	400	14.10	1¾ cups	60.15%
Salt	13	0.45	2¼ tsp.	1.95%
TOTAL FORMULA	1,078	38.00		162.10%
Rye flour for dusting	As needed			

1. Combine the flour, warm water, and salt in the mixer and use the dough hook at low (KA2) speed until they develop into a moderately stiff dough, 5–6 minutes.

2. Turn the dough onto an unfloured work surface and knead briefly to bring together, then divide into twelve 85 g/3 oz. pieces. Roll each into a ball.

3. Dust the dough balls and work surface generously with rye flour and use your palm to press the dough into a disk about ½ inch/1.25 cm thick. Use a rolling pin to roll each piece into a round roughly 8 inches/20 cm in diameter and ⅛ inch/0.3 cm or less thick. As you finish each piece, cover it with a lightly dampened towel to prevent drying.

4. Heat a cast-iron or aluminum griddle over medium-high heat and bake each bread until it bubbles, about 1 minute, then turn it and bake the other side for 1–2 minutes. Flip the bread again and, while baking, press it with a dish towel until it puffs up, about 30 seconds. Wrap in a clean towel and serve warm.

Sour Ring Bread

Hapanleipä

FINLAND   This is the daily loaf of modern Finland. Its circular shape, center hole, and firm texture recall the ring breads (*ruisreikäleipä*) of western Finland, while its assertive sour and dense, chewy crumb bespeak the Russian-influenced *ruislimppu* loaves of eastern Finland. This is the bread that's traditionally served with Finnish pea soup (*hernekeitto*), beef, lamb, and pork boil (*karjalanpaisti*), and morels stewed in buttermilk (*korvasienimuhennos*). Here in America, try it with smoked salmon, trout *amandine*, or cream of mushroom soup.

RYE %:	**100%**
STAGES:	**Sponge, final dough**
LEAVEN:	**Rye sour culture**
START TO FINISH:	**13–16 hours**
HANDS-ON TIME:	**30–40 minutes**
YIELD:	**Two 2 lb./900 g loaves**

SPONGE (DAY 1, EVENING)

INGREDIENT	GRAMS	OUNCES	VOLUME	BAKER'S PERCENTAGE
Medium rye meal	110	3.90	1 cup	100%
Warm (105°F/41°C) water	275	9.70	1 cup	250%
Rye sour culture (see page 35)	10	0.35	½ cup	9%

1. Mix the sponge ingredients by hand until incorporated, cover, and ferment at room temperature (68–72°F/20–22°C) overnight, 10–12 hours. The sponge will be very bubbly, have a clean sour smell, and will have doubled in volume.

recipe continues

FINAL DOUGH (DAY 2, MORNING)

INGREDIENT	GRAMS	OUNCES	VOLUME
Sponge	395	13.95	Use all
Warm (105°F/41°C) water	660	23.30	3 cups less 1 Tbs.
Salt	14	0.50	2 tsp.
Medium rye flour	900	31.75	7 cups
Flour for dusting	As needed		

2. Combine the sponge, water, and salt in the mixer. Use the dough hook at low (KA2) speed, scraping down the bowl as necessary, to mix until blended, then add the rye flour slowly until the dough is fully developed, 6–8 minutes.

3. Turn the dough onto a well-floured work surface and divide it into two pieces weighing approximately 1.0 kg/2.2 lb. each. Shape each piece into a ball and use a rolling pin to roll into a circle about 10 inches/25 cm in diameter and 1 inch/2.5 cm thick. Use a glass or biscuit cutter to remove a circle of dough from the center and pat the excess into the ring of dough or bake it separately. Place on a well-floured peel, if using a baking stone, or on a parchment-lined sheet pan. Cover and proof at room temperature until visibly expanded, 2–3 hours.

4. Preheat the oven to 425°F/220°C with the baking surface in the upper third. Dock the surface of each loaf thoroughly and evenly to a depth of at least ¼ inch/0.6 cm with a fork, chopstick, or docking wheel and bake until the crust is deep brown and the internal temperature is at least 198°F/92°C, 40–50 minutes. Transfer to a rack and let stand for 2–3 days for best flavor.

BAKER'S PERCENTAGES

INGREDIENT	G	%
Medium rye flour	1,010	100.00%
Water	935	92.57%
Salt	14	1.39%
Rye sour culture	10	0.99%
TOTAL FORMULA	1,969	194.95%
Total flour prefermented	110	10.89%

This traditional **Sour Ring Bread** is the daily bread of modern Finland, featuring a dense crumb, a rye sweetness, and an assertive sour finish.

Sweden's bakeries offer many versions of **limpa**. This one, topped with sliced hardboiled egg and bristling sardines, showcases the sweetness of rye and light molasses syrup, perfumed with the fragrance of anise, fennel, caraway, and coriander.

Sweet Limpa

Siraplimpa

There are many different variations of the classic Swedish *limpa*: they can be made of mixed wheat and rye or exclusively rye; they can be spiced with orange peel or zest, anise, fennel, or all of these. This version is built on a yeast-leavened straight dough, making it both quick and easy. Milk tenderizes the crumb and a bouquet of fragrant spices, light molasses, and 100% rye produce a loaf that's sweet and richly aromatic.

Every year I take two loaves of this bread to the Christmas Eve open house hosted by a friend of ours who's of Swedish descent. One loaf goes on the groaning board, where it disappears quickly, paired with everything from hummus to capicola. The other gets made into French toast for the family's Christmas morning breakfast. Rarely, if ever, has the bread made it to Boxing Day (December 26).

RYE %:	**100%**
STAGES:	**Straight dough**
LEAVEN:	**Yeast**
START TO FINISH:	**2 hours**
HANDS-ON TIME:	**25 minutes**
YIELD:	**Two 1½ lb./680 g loaves**

recipe continues

DOUGH

INGREDIENT	GRAMS	OUNCES	VOLUME	BAKER'S PERCENTAGE
Unsalted butter	50	1.75	3½ Tbs.	5.88%
Whole milk, at room temperature (68–72°F/20–22°C)	400	14.10	1⅔ cups	47.06%
Warm (105°F/41°C) water	100	3.55	⅜ cup	11.76%
Light molasses, malt syrup, or light corn syrup	150	5.30	½ cup	17.65%
Salt	12	0.40	2 tsp.	1.41%
Caraway seed, toasted and ground	3	0.10	1¼ tsp.	0.35%
Fennel seed, toasted and ground	2	0.05	1 tsp.	0.24%
Aniseed, toasted and ground	2	0.05	½ tsp.	0.24%
Coriander seed, toasted and ground	2	0.05	1 tsp.	0.12%
Medium rye flour	850	30.00	6⅔ cups	100.00%
Instant yeast	8	0.30	2 tsp.	0.94%
TOTAL FORMULA	1,578	55.65		185.65%
Flour for dusting	As needed			

1. In a saucepan, melt the butter over medium heat, then add the milk, water, syrup, salt, and spices and warm to 105°F/41°C.

2. Put the flour and yeast in the mixer, add the milk mixture, and use the dough hook at low (KA2) speed to mix into a firm, smooth dough, about 5 minutes. Cover and ferment at room temperature (68–72°F/20–22°C), until the dough has visibly expanded, 40–45 minutes.

3. Turn the dough, which will be only slightly sticky and very easy to handle, onto a lightly floured work surface and divide it into two pieces weighing about 790 g/28 oz. each. Shape each piece into an oval loaf. Set the loaves on a well-floured peel, if using a baking stone, or a parchment-lined sheet pan. Cover and proof at room temperature until the first cracks appear on the surface of the loaves, 30–40 minutes.

4. Preheat the oven to 400°F/200°C with the baking surface in the middle. Bake until the loaf thumps when tapped with a finger and the internal temperature is at least 198°F/92°C, 35–40 minutes. Transfer to a rack and cool thoroughly before slicing.

Rye-Raisin Scones

Rågkakor med Russin

`SWEDEN` People don't normally associate rye and scones, but they should. These scones have the richness of wheat-flour scones, but not in the same way. Wheat scones contain lots of fat; except for the milk, these are fat-free. Instead, they get their richness from the combination of rye meal and raisins. Texturally they're moist, smooth, and chewy, with a flavor profile that's sweet-sour and nutty. For a different taste, substitute coarsely chopped walnuts, chocolate chips, or dried blueberries or cranberries for the raisins.

We like them topped with butter or jam for Sunday and holiday brunch. Any that go uneaten can be kept in plastic bags—they'll stay fresh for up to a week—and popped into the toaster for a quick and satisfying weekday breakfast.

RYE %:	**53%**
STAGES:	**Straight dough**
LEAVEN:	**Yeast**
START TO FINISH:	**2½ hours**
HANDS-ON TIME:	**25–30 minutes**
YIELD:	**Sixteen 2 oz./56 g scones**

DOUGH

INGREDIENT	GRAMS	OUNCES	VOLUME	BAKER'S PERCENTAGE
Water	225	7.95	1 cup	45.00%
Whole milk	150	5.35	⅔ cup	30.00%
Instant yeast	10	0.35	1 Tbs.	2.00%
Coarse rye meal	262	9.25	1⅔ cups	52.50%
Bread flour	238	8.40	1¾ cups	47.50%
Salt	6	0.20	1 tsp.	1.20%
Raisins	70	2.45	½ cup	14.00%
TOTAL FORMULA	962	33.95		192.20%
Total flour	500	17.65		100.00%
Flour for dusting	As needed			

recipe continues

1. Warm the water and milk to body temperature (100°F/38°C) and dissolve the yeast in it. Combine the dry ingredients in a mixing bowl, add the liquids, and mix by hand until the dough is fully developed. Add the raisins and continue mixing until evenly blended.

2. Cover and ferment at room temperature (68–72°F/20–22°C) until the dough has visibly expanded, 30–45 minutes.

3. Turn the dough, which will be very sticky, onto a well-floured work surface and use floured hands to bring it together. Divide into two pieces, each weighing about 480 g/ 17 oz., and shape each into a ball.

4. Place the dough balls on a parchment-lined sheet pan and use floured hands to press each into a disk about 8 inches/20 cm in diameter and ½ inch/1.3 cm thick. Dock with a fork, chopstick, or docking wheel to a depth of ¼–½ inch/0.6–1.25 cm, cover, and proof at room temperature until slightly expanded, 40–50 minutes.

5. Preheat the oven to 485°F/250°C with the baking surface in the middle. Use a sharp knife, pizza wheel, or dough scraper to cut each disk into eight wedges, then bake until the crust is light brown and the internal temperature is at least 198°F/92°C, 15–17 minutes. Serve warm.

Variation:

Add 3 g/1 tsp. toasted anise, fennel, or caraway seed and replace the raisins with an equal volume of coarsely chopped walnuts.

The rustic crunch of coarse rye meal combines with the sweet softness of raisins in these quick and easy Scandinavian **Rye-Raisin Scones**. Plum preserves give them added tang.

Slow-Baked Finnish Rye

Jälkiuunileipä

FINLAND In northern Finland, bread baking took place only twice a year—coinciding with the coming of the spring thaw and autumn rains that powered the mills—and lasted for weeks on end. When the main baking was done, the bakers mixed their leftover sour sponge with whatever odds and ends of flour they had on hand. This they placed in their wood-fired ovens, to bake slowly as the fires died down and the ovens gradually cooled. They called their bread *jälkiuunileipä*, "after-bake loaf."

Eastern Finnish breads show a strong Russian-Baltic influence, and, like so many breads of the region, this dense loaf contrasts an assertive sour against the sweet notes of malted rye, whole wheat or spelt, and buckwheat. The dough's abundant sugars caramelize to deep brown during the long low-temperature bake, which also produces its open, tender crumb and thick, chewy crust. This is a bread that shines, no matter whether it's paired with ripe cheeses and cured meats or veal marsala and poached salmon.

RYE %:	73%
STAGES:	**2-stage sponge, final dough**
LEAVEN:	**Rye sour culture, yeast**
START TO FINISH:	**25–30 hours**
HANDS-ON TIME:	**30–40 minutes**
YIELD:	**One 3 lb./1.35 kg loaf**

STAGE 1 SPONGE (DAY 1, MORNING)

INGREDIENT	GRAMS	OUNCES	VOLUME	BAKER'S PERCENTAGE
Medium rye flour	152	5.35	1¼ cups	100%
Warm (105°F/41°C) water	152	5.35	⅔ cup	100%
Rye sour culture (see page 35)	16	0.55	1¼ Tbs.	11%

1. Mix the Stage 1 ingredients by hand until incorporated, cover, and ferment at room temperature (68–72°F/20–22°C) overnight, 10–12 hours. The sponge will be very bubbly, have a clean sour smell, and will have doubled in volume.

STAGE 2 SPONGE (DAY 1, EVENING)

INGREDIENT	GRAMS	OUNCES	VOLUME	BAKER'S PERCENTAGE
Medium rye flour	140	4.95	1⅛ cups	56%
Whole-wheat or whole-spelt flour	110	3.90	1 cup	44%
Warm (105°F/41°C) water	400	14.10	1⅔ cups	160%
Instant yeast	3	0.10	¾ tsp.	1%
Red rye malt (see page 42)	120	4.25	¾ cup	48%
Stage 1 sponge	320	11.25	Use all	128%

2. Add the Stage 2 sponge ingredients to the Stage 1 sponge and mix by hand to incorporate. Cover and ferment at room temperature overnight, 10–12 hours. The sponge will be very fragrant and bubbly and will have visibly expanded.

FINAL DOUGH (DAY 2, MORNING)

INGREDIENT	GRAMS	OUNCES	VOLUME
Stage 2 sponge	1,093	38.55	Use all
Salt	10	0.35	1⅔ tsp.
Honey	32	1.15	1½ Tbs.
Buckwheat flour	128	4.50	1 cup
Medium rye flour	120	4.25	1 cup
Vegetable shortening for pan	As needed.		

3. Combine the Stage 2 sponge, salt, and honey in the mixer and use the paddle at low (KA 2) speed to mix until blended, 2–3 minutes. Gradually add the flours and continue mixing until the dough forms a soft, sticky mass, 8–10 minutes.

4. Use a plastic dough scraper and wet hands to transfer the dough into a well-greased 9-by-4-by-4-inch/23-by-10-by-10 cm Pullman loaf pan or 9-by-5-by-3-inch/23-by-13-by-8 cm loaf pan. Cover and proof at room temperature until the dough approaches the rim of the pans, 60–75 minutes.

recipe continues

5. Preheat the oven to 225°F/105°C with the baking surface in the middle. Cover the loaf pan securely with lightly greased aluminum foil (leaving some slack for the loaf to expand) and bake 6 hours, then remove the foil and bake until the loaf thumps when tapped with a finger and the internal temperature is at least 198°F/92°C, 60–75 minutes longer. Remove from the pan and transfer to a rack, wrap in a clean towel, and let rest 24–48 hours before slicing.

BAKER'S PERCENTAGES

INGREDIENT	G	%
TOTAL FLOUR	650	100.00%
Medium rye flour	412	63.38%
Buckwheat flour	128	19.69%
Whole-wheat/spelt flour	110	16.92%
Water	552	84.92%
Salt	10	1.54%
Instant yeast	3	0.46%
Red rye malt	120	18.46%
Honey	32	4.92%
Rye sour culture	16	2.46%
TOTAL FORMULA	1,383	212.77%
Total flour prefermented	402	61.85%

Buttery Crispbread

Knäckebröd med Smör

SWEDEN Rye crispbread is one of those Scandinavian standards for which recipes abound. Of the dozens I've seen, I like this one best: it's made with 100% rye, of which 70% is coarse rye meal, giving the crackers a rustic and toothsome crunch. The base flavor is pure rye, sweetened and made lighter by the butter. It's also flexible enough to allow for a wide range of taste and textural variations. The addition of cumin, caraway, fennel, dill, and/or anise, individually or in combination, creates nuances that can take a single topping—aged cheddar cheese, for example—in many different directions. Flaxseed or sesame seed can add additional layers of richness and crunch. Best of all, these crackers keep fresh for months stored in plastic—that is, if they last that long.

RYE %:	**100%**
STAGES:	**Sponge, final dough**
LEAVEN:	**Yeast**
START TO FINISH:	**2 hours**
HANDS-ON TIME:	**30–45 minutes**
YIELD:	**About 4 dozen crackers**

SPONGE

INGREDIENT	GRAMS	OUNCES	VOLUME	BAKER'S PERCENTAGE
Coarse rye meal	540	19.05	3½ cups	100%
Warm (105°F/41°C) water	425	15.00	1¾ cups	79%
Instant yeast	16	0.55	1¼ tsp.	3%
Sugar	20	0.70	5 tsp.	4%
Unsalted butter, at room temperature (68–72°F/20–22°C)	75	2.65	⅓ cup	14%
Salt	8	0.30	1½ tsp.	1%
Flax or sesame seed (optional)	50	1.75	⅓ cup	7%
Cumin, caraway, fennel, dill, or anise seed, toasted (optional)	6	0.20	1 Tbs.	1%

recipe continues

WINE SOAKER (DAY 1, EVENING)

INGREDIENT	GRAMS	OUNCES	VOLUME	BAKER'S PERCENTAGE
Light-bodied white wine—e.g., riesling or pinot grigio	50	1.75	¼ cup	100%
Candied lemon peel, diced	50	1.75	¼ cup	100%
Candied orange peel, diced	50	1.75	¼ cup	100%

2. In a separate bowl, combine the wine soaker ingredients, cover, and let stand at room temperature overnight, 10–12 hours.

FINAL DOUGH (DAY 2, MORNING)

INGREDIENT	GRAMS	OUNCES	VOLUME
Ground aniseed	3	0.10	1 tsp.
Ground fennel seed	3	0.10	1 tsp.
Medium rye flour	150	5.30	1¼ cup
AP flour	100	3.50	¾ cup
Warm (105°F/41°C) water	255	9.00	1 cup + 2 Tbs.
Sugar	25	0.90	2 Tbs.
Salt	14	0.50	2¼ tsp
Instant yeast	8	0.30	1 Tbs.
Vegetable oil	14	0.50	1 Tbs.
Grated lemon zest	3	0.10	1 tsp.
Grated orange zest	3	0.10	1 tsp.
Ground cinnamon	3	0.10	¾ tsp.
Ground cloves	1	0.05	¼ tsp.
Grated nutmeg	1	0.05	¼ tsp.
Rum-honey soaker	1,220	43.05	Use all
Wine soaker	150	5.25	Use all
Flour for dusting	As needed		
Candied fruit and nuts for garnish (optional)	As needed		

3. Combine the ground anise and fennel seed with the flours, warm water, sugar, salt, yeast, and vegetable oil in the mixer. Use the dough hook at low-medium (KA4) speed, scraping down the bowl as necessary, until the dough, which will be soft and sticky, forms high-walled ridges around the beater, 6–8 minutes. Add the citrus zest, cinnamon, cloves, and nutmeg and mix until evenly blended, 2–3 minutes. Leave the dough in the mixer bowl, cover and ferment at room temperature until it has doubled in volume, 60–75 minutes.

4. Add both soakers, along with any remaining liquid to the dough and use the dough hook at low (KA2) speed to blend into a soft, sticky mass, with just enough dough to hold the fruits and nuts together. Use a bench knife or plastic dough scraper to divide the dough into three pieces, each weighing about 25 oz./630 g, and shape each into a flattened oval loaf about 8-by-4 inches/20-by-10 cm. Set the loaves 1–2 inches/2.5–5 cm apart on a parchment-lined sheet pan. If desired, garnish with blanched almonds, walnuts, and/or candied fruits.

WASH

INGREDIENT	GRAMS	OUNCES	VOLUME
Warm (105°F/41°C) water	56	2.00	¼ cup
Honey	42	1.50	2 Tbs.

5. Preheat the oven to 340°F/170°C with the baking surface in the middle. Brush the *zelten* generously with the wash and bake until the crust is lightly browned and the internal temperature is at least 198°F/92°C, 40–45 minutes. Transfer to a rack and cool thoroughly, then wrap the loaves tightly in plastic and season at room temperature for at least 2 weeks before slicing.

recipe continues

BAKER'S PERCENTAGES

INGREDIENT	G	%
TOTAL FLOUR	250	100.00%
Medium rye flour	150	60.00%
AP flour	100	40.00%
Water	200	80.00%
Salt	15	6.00%
Instant yeast	8	3.20%
Dried figs	500	200.00%
Raisins	370	148.00%
Tree nuts	120	48.00%
Pine nuts	120	48.00%
Candied citrus peel	100	40.00%
Honey	70	28.00%
White wine	66	20.00%
Rum	40	16.00%
Sugar	25	10.00%
Vegetable oil	15	6.00%
Spices	5	2.00%
Citrus zest	4	1.60%
TOTAL FORMULA	1,908	763.20%

This **South Tyrolean Christmas Zelten** from the town of Bolzano in the Italian Alps began as an ordinary rye bread, to which a handful of dried fruit and nuts was added. Over time, it became one of Italy's lushest, most flavorful, and least known holiday breads.

Sauerkraut Bread

Sauerkrautbrot

GERMANY Sauerkraut breads are a tradition in central Europe. Most of them, however, are wheat based. This loaf adds the nutty spiciness of 63% rye and a caraway edge to the sweet and sour of the fermented cabbage. The crumb is close and tender with a thick, chewy crust. The dough is easy to work and forgiving. This is a bread that pairs exceptionally well with a generous filling of hot pastrami or corned beef and brown mustard.

RYE %:	**63%**
STAGES:	**Sponge, soaker, final dough**
LEAVEN:	**Rye sour culture, yeast**
START TO FINISH:	**16–20 hours**
HANDS-ON TIME:	**30–40 minutes**
YIELD:	**Two 1¾ lb./800 g loaves**

SPONGE (DAY 1, EVENING)

INGREDIENT	GRAMS	OUNCES	VOLUME	BAKER'S PERCENTAGE
Medium rye flour	207	7.30	1⅔ cups	100%
Warm (105°F/41°C) water	165	5.80	⅔ cup	80%
Rye sour culture (see page 35)	20	0.70	5 tsp.	10%

1. Mix the sponge ingredients by hand until incorporated, cover, and ferment at room temperature (68°–72°F/20–22°C) overnight, 10–12 hours. The sponge will be very bubbly, have a clean sour smell, and will have doubled in volume.

SOAKER (DAY 2, MORNING)

INGREDIENT	GRAMS	OUNCES	VOLUME	BAKER'S PERCENTAGE
Fine rye meal	122	4.30	⅔ cup	100%
Warm (105°F/41°C) water	61	2.15	¼ cup	50%
Sauerkraut (see Note), drained	243	8.60	2¾ cups	200%
Ground caraway seed	8	0.30	4 tsp.	6%

2. In a separate container, mix the soaker ingredients by hand until well integrated, cover, and let stand in a warm area (80°F/27°C) 3–4 hours.

FINAL DOUGH (DAY 2, AFTERNOON)

INGREDIENT	GRAMS	OUNCES	VOLUME
Sponge	392	13.80	Use all
Soaker	434	15.35	Use all
AP flour	348	12.25	2⅔ cups
White rye flour	261	9.20	1⅞ cups
Warm (105°F/41°C) water	313	11.05	1⅓ cups
Salt	16	0.55	2⅔ tsp.
Instant yeast	7	0.25	1¾ tsp.
Flour for dusting	As needed		

3. Combine the sponge, soaker, flours, warm water, salt, and yeast in the mixer and use the dough hook at low (KA2) speed to mix until the dough comes together and cleans the sides of the bowl, 8–10 minutes. Cover and ferment at room temperature until the dough doubles in volume, 45–60 minutes.

4. Turn the dough onto a well-floured work surface. It will be soft and somewhat sticky but becomes very easy to work with floured hands. Knead the dough back to its original volume and divide it into two pieces, each weighing about 890 g/31 oz. Shape each piece into a round loaf, flour the smooth side generously, and place seam side up in well-floured bread forms (see page 72) or cloth-lined baskets. Cover and proof at room temperature until the surface of the dough shows cracks or broken bubbles, 30–45 minutes.

recipe continues

5. Preheat the oven to 485°F/250°C with a steam pan (see page 76) and the baking surface in the middle. Flip the loaves onto a well-floured peel, if using a baking stone, or onto a parchment-lined sheet pan and bake with steam for 3 minutes. Remove the steam pan, lower the oven temperature to 390°F/200°C, and bake until the loaf thumps when tapped with a finger and the internal temperature is at least 198°F/92°C, 50–55 minutes. Transfer to a rack and cool thoroughly before slicing.

Note: Because the rye sponge produces the delicate acid finish I prefer in this bread, I use mild Polish sauerkraut—available at specialty and ethnic groceries. For stronger, more front-of-the-mouth flavor, use German or domestic American sauerkraut.

BAKER'S PERCENTAGES

INGREDIENT	G	%
TOTAL FLOUR	938	100.00%
AP flour	348	37.12%
White rye flour	261	27.82%
Medium rye flour	207	22.08%
Fine rye meal	122	12.98%
Water	478	50.99%
Salt	16	1.67%
Instant yeast	7	0.74%
Sauerkraut	243	25.97%
Soaker water	61	6.49%
Rye sour culture	20	2.13%
Caraway seed	8	0.83%
TOTAL FORMULA	1,771	188.82%
Total flour prefermented	207	22.08%

"Lifted" Country Boule

Ausgehobenes Bauernbrot

AUSTRIA This rustic Austrian bread gets its name from "lifting" the dough directly into the oven after a short bulk fermentation. It uses the Berlin One-Stage Quick Sponge (*Berliner Kurzsauer*) method (see page 52), which makes this one of the few fully realized sour ryes that can go from start to finish in a single day. If it's not possible to use the quick sponge, use a basic one-stage overnight sponge (see page 52) instead.

The loaves are small—6–8 inches/15–20 cm in diameter and dense—with a close, very tender crumb. The nicely balanced sour doesn't overwhelm but complements the rye's spicy nuttiness. As I chewed this bread for the first time, I was also pleasantly surprised by the subtle but insistent sweetness of the whole-grain wheat that clearly came through—and which immediately became something I looked forward to in my next bite. In all, this is a bread whose pronounced yet not overwhelming flavor profile pairs beautifully with both mild Alpine cheeses like Emmenthaler or Appenzeller and strong-flavored charcuterie.

RYE %:	**75%**
STAGES:	**Yeast wheat sponge, rye sponge, soaker, final dough**
LEAVEN:	**Rye sour culture, yeast**
START TO FINISH:	**6–7 hours**
HANDS-ON TIME:	**45–60 minutes**
YIELD:	**Three 1¼ lb./550 g loaves**

WHEAT SPONGE

INGREDIENT	GRAMS	OUNCES	VOLUME	BAKER'S PERCENTAGE
Whole-wheat flour	140	4.95	1⅓ cups	100%
Warm (105°F/41°C) water	140	4.95	⅝ cup	100%
Instant yeast	2	0.05	⅓ tsp.	1%

recipe continues

1. Mix the sponge ingredients by hand until incorporated, cover and ferment at room temperature (68–72°F/20–22°C) for 3½–4 hours. The sponge will have tripled in volume and begun to fall back on itself.

RYE SPONGE

INGREDIENT	GRAMS	OUNCES	VOLUME	BAKER'S PERCENTAGE
Dark rye flour	300	10.60	3¼ cups	83%
White rye flour	60	2.10	⅜ cup	17%
Warm (105°F/41°C) water	390	13.75	1⅜ cups	108%
Rye sour culture (see page 35)	70	2.45	⅓ cup	19%

2. Mix the rye sponge ingredients by hand until incorporated into a stiff dough. Cover and place in a warm oven or proofing box to ferment at 95°F/35°C for 3½–4 hours. The sponge will have a clean sour smell and will have visibly expanded, showing a webwork of cracks on the surface.

SOAKER

INGREDIENT	GRAMS	OUNCES	VOLUME	BAKER'S PERCENTAGE
Stale rye bread	50	1.75	½ cup less 1 Tbs.	100%
Warm (105°F/41°C) water	100	3.55	½ cup less 1 Tbs.	200%

3. Break up the stale rye bread and moisten it evenly with the water. Cover and let stand at room temperature for 3½–4 hours.

FINAL DOUGH

INGREDIENT	GRAMS	OUNCES	VOLUME
Soaker	150	5.30	Use all
Rye sponge	820	28.90	Use all
Wheat sponge	282	9.95	Use all

Medium rye flour	180	6.35	1¼ cups
White rye flour	60	2.10	½ cup less 1 Tbs.
Bread flour	60	2.10	½ cup less 1 Tbs.
Salt	20	0.70	3⅓ tsp.
Unsalted butter	30	1.05	⅛ cup (¼ stick)
Caraway, fennel, or anise seed for topping (optional)	6	0.20	1 Tbs.
Medium rye flour for dusting	As needed		

4. Mash the soaker with a fork and combine it with the sponges, flours, salt, and butter in the mixer. To avoid flying flour, use the paddle at lowest (KA1) speed until the dough starts to blend, then increase the speed to low (KA2) and mix, scraping down the bowl as needed, until a firm, sticky dough develops, about 6 minutes. Increase the speed to low-medium (KA4) and mix for 1 minute more, then cover and ferment at room temperature until the dough has visibly expanded and its surface shows cracks or bubbles, about 60 minutes.

5. Turn the dough onto a lightly floured work surface and divide it into three pieces weighing about 500 g/18 oz. each. Use floured hands to shape them into rough rounds and place on a well-floured peel, if using a baking stone, or on a parchment-lined sheet pan. Brush each loaf with water and top with the seeds if desired.

6. Preheat the oven to 485°F/250°C with a steam pan (see page 76) and the baking surface in the middle. Bake with steam for 5 minutes, remove the steam pan, and bake for another 5 minutes, then lower the temperature to 385°F/200°C and bake until the crust thumps when tapped with a finger and the internal temperature is at least 198°F/92°C, 25–30 minutes. Transfer to a rack and cool thoroughly before slicing.

recipe continues

BAKER'S PERCENTAGES

INGREDIENT	G	%
TOTAL FLOUR	800	100.00%
Dark rye flour	240	30.00%
Medium rye flour	120	15.00%
White rye flour	240	30.00%
Whole-wheat flour	140	17.50%
Bread flour	60	7.50%
Water	530	66.25%
Salt	20	2.50%
Instant yeast	2	0.25%
Soaker water	100	12.50%
Stale rye bread	50	6.25%
Butter	30	3.75%
TOTAL FORMULA	1,532	191.50%
Total flour prefermented	500	62.50%

Bavarian Rye

Schnaitsee Roggenbrot

GERMANY This fine-textured country loaf comes from the Alpine foothills of southeastern Bavaria, where the wheat-, spelt- and rye-growing regions meet. It's a well-balanced bread, with a fragrant, nutty taste and subtle tang enhanced by its caraway-coriander edge. It has a firm, close crumb that surprises with chewy nuggets of rye meal and the crunch of flaxseed. This bread pairs nicely with veined cheeses like Stilton or Roquefort and with Bavarian specialties like roast pork, red cabbage, and Bavarian dumplings (*spätzle*), accompanied by a glass of chilled wheat beer (*hefeweizen*).

RYE %:	**63%**
STAGES:	**2-stage sponge, soaker, final dough**
LEAVEN:	**Rye sour culture**
START TO FINISH:	**30–32 hours**
HANDS-ON TIME:	**45–60 minutes**
YIELD:	**One 3 lb./1.35 kg loaf**

STAGE 1 SPONGE (DAY 1, MORNING)

INGREDIENT	GRAMS	OUNCES	VOLUME	BAKER'S PERCENTAGE
Medium rye flour	35	1.25	¼ cup	100%
Warm (105°F/41°C) water	60	2.10	¼ cup	171%
Rye sour culture (see page 35)	5	0.20	1 tsp.	14%

1. Mix the Stage 1 ingredients by hand until incorporated, cover, and ferment at room temperature (68–72°F/20–22°C), 10–12 hours. The sponge will be very bubbly, have a clean sour smell, and will have doubled in volume.

recipe continues

STAGE 2 SPONGE (DAY 1, EVENING)

INGREDIENT	GRAMS	OUNCES	VOLUME	BAKER'S PERCENTAGE
Medium rye flour	115	4.05	1 cup	100%
Warm (105°F/41°C) water	55	1.95	¼ cup	48%
Salt	2	0.05	¼ tsp.	4%
Caraway seed	5	0.15	2 tsp.	2%
Stage 1 sponge	100	3.55	Use all	87%

2. Add the Stage 2 ingredients to the Stage 1 sponge and mix by hand to incorporate. Cover and ferment at room temperature overnight, 10–12 hours. The sponge will have doubled in volume and begun to fall back.

SOAKER (DAY 1, EVENING)

INGREDIENT	GRAMS	OUNCES	VOLUME	BAKER'S PERCENTAGE
Coarse rye meal or steel-cut oats	60	2.10	⅓ cup	100%
Warm (105°F/41°C) water	150	5.30	⅔ cup	250%

3. In a separate container, combine the soaker ingredients, cover, and let stand at room temperature overnight, 10–12 hours.

FINAL DOUGH (DAY 2, MORNING)

INGREDIENT	GRAMS	OUNCES	VOLUME
Stage 2 sponge	277	9.75	Use all
Soaker	210	7.40	Use all
Medium rye flour	292	10.30	2¼ cups
First clear or high-gluten flour	292	10.30	2 cups
Warm (105°F/41°C) water	292	10.30	1¼ cups
Salt	15	0.50	2½ tsp.
Flaxseed	13	0.45	1¼ Tbs.
Coriander seed, toasted and ground	4	0.10	1⅔ tsp.
Flour for dusting	As needed		

4. Combine the Stage 2 sponge, soaker, flours, water, salt, and seeds in the mixer and use the paddle at low (KA2) speed to mix until the dough forms a shaggy mass, 2–3 minutes. Switch to the dough hook and continue mixing until the dough, which will be dense and sticky, is well blended, 6–8 minutes. Cover and ferment at room temperature until doubled in volume, 2–4 hours.

5. Turn the dough onto a well-floured work surface and use floured hands to shape it into a large round loaf. Place the loaf seam side down on a well-floured peel, if using a baking stone, or on a parchment-lined sheet pan. Cover and proof at room temperature until the loaf has visibly expanded and shows cracks on the surface, 45–60 minutes.

6. Preheat the oven to 500°F/260°C with the baking surface in the upper third and a steam pan (see page 76) on a lower shelf. Reduce the temperature to 485°F/250°C and bake with steam for 10 minutes, then remove the steam pan, lower the oven temperature to 400°F/205°C, and bake for 20 minutes. Lower the temperature again, to 300°F/150°C, and bake until the loaf thumps when tapped with a finger and the internal temperature is at least 198°F/92°C, 20–25 minutes. Transfer to a rack and cool at least 24 hours before cutting.

BAKER'S PERCENTAGES

INGREDIENT	G	%
TOTAL FLOUR	794	100.00%
Medium rye flour	442	55.67%
First clear flour	292	36.78%
Coarse rye meal	60	7.56%
Water	407	51.26%
Salt	15	1.89%
Soaker water	150	18.89%
Flaxseed	13	1.64%
Caraway seed	5	0.63%
Coriander seed	4	0.50%
Rye sour culture	5	0.63%
TOTAL FORMULA	1,393	175.45%
Total flour prefermented	150	18.89%

Black Bread of Val d'Aosta

Pan Ner'

ITALY Wheat won't grow in the Italian Alps, making rye the grain, if not of choice, then certainly of necessity. In times past, communal baking took place a few times a year—to coincide, perhaps, with the harvests of summer and winter rye or with the spring and autumn floods that powered the mills. The baked loaves hardened on racks called *ratele* and were cut with a *copapan* ("bread cutter"), which had a hooked tip that fit into an eyelet on the bread board, so that it worked like a paper cutter. Today, even though wheat flour is now widely available, *pan ner'* is a South Tyrol tradition that's celebrated in the *Couetta Pan Ner'*, a festival that takes place annually in the village of Marine.

This recipe closely follows the traditional practice of leavening the bread with rye sour culture only. The result is a dense, tight-crumbed loaf that combines both sweet and sour notes, complemented by the sweet crunch of sesame and sunflower seeds. Try this bread with an aged prosciutto or a nutty Alpine cheese like Beaufort, Fontina, or fenugreek-spiced Sapsago cheese, finely grated and mixed with sweet butter.

RYE %:	**67%**
STAGES:	**Sponge, final dough**
LEAVEN:	**Rye sour culture**
START TO FINISH:	**16–20 hours**
HANDS-ON TIME:	**25–30 minutes**
YIELD:	**Two 1¾ lb./800 g loaves**

SPONGE (DAY 1, EVENING)

INGREDIENT	GRAMS	OUNCES	VOLUME	BAKER'S PERCENTAGE
Medium rye flour	70	2.50	½ cup	100%
Warm (105°F/41°C) water	70	2.50	¼ cup + 1 Tbs.	100%
Rye sour culture (see page 35)	10	0.35	2½ tsp.	15%

1. Mix the sponge ingredients by hand until incorporated, cover, and ferment at room temperature (68–72°F/20–22°C) overnight, 10–12 hours. The sponge will be very bubbly, have a clean sour smell, and will have doubled in volume.

FINAL DOUGH (DAY 2, MORNING)

INGREDIENT	GRAMS	OUNCES	VOLUME
Sponge	150	5.30	Use all
Medium rye flour	650	23.00	5 cups
AP flour	350	12.35	2¾ cups
Warm (105°F/41°C) water	550	19.40	2⅓ cups
Salt	10	0.35	1½ tsp.
Sesame seed	20	0.70	⅛ cup
Sunflower seeds	20	0.70	⅛ cup
Flaxseed	5	0.20	1½ tsp.
Flour for dusting			

2. Combine the sponge, flours, warm water, salt, and seeds in the mixer and use the dough hook at low (KA2) speed until the dough is fully integrated and leaves the sides of the bowl, 8–10 minutes. Cover and ferment at room temperature until doubled in volume, 4–6 hours.

3. Turn the dough onto a lightly floured work surface, knead it back to its original volume, then divide into two pieces, each weighing about 875 g/31 oz. Shape each into a round or oval loaf and place on well-floured peel, if using a baking stone, or a parchment lined baking sheet. Cover and proof at room temperature until doubled in size, 60–75 minutes.

4. Preheat the oven to 425°F/220°C with the baking surface in the middle. Slash round loaves with a cross and oblong loaves diagonally to a depth of ¼–½ inch/0.6–1.25 cm, then bake until the loaf thumps when tapped with a finger and the internal temperature is at least 198°F/92°C, 40–45 minutes. Transfer to a rack and cool thoroughly before slicing.

recipe continues

BAKER'S PERCENTAGES

INGREDIENT	G	%
TOTAL FLOUR	1,070	100.00%
Medium rye flour	720	67.29%
AP flour	350	32.71%
Water	620	57.94%
Salt	10	0.93%
Sesame seed	20	1.87%
Sunflower seeds	20	1.87%
Flaxseed	5	0.47%
Rye sour culture	10	0.93%
TOTAL FORMULA	1,755	164.01%
Total flour prefermented	70	6.54%

Rye Bites

Schuastabuam

GERMANY These feather-light minirolls are easy and delicious and, unlike so many rye breads, take only an hour or two from start to finish. They're built on a straight dough that accelerates the yeast fermentation with sugar, requiring only a short half-hour proof. The crust is crisp, and the sweet crumb is open and tender. Consider these tasty bites for your next dinner party or for a last-minute change of pace from your usual breakfast breads. They also make great two-bite slider rolls.

RYE %:	67%
STAGES:	**Straight dough**
LEAVEN:	**Yeast**
START TO FINISH:	**1–1½ hours**
HANDS-ON TIME:	**20–25 minutes**
YIELD:	**Two dozen 1¼ oz./35 g rolls**

DOUGH

INGREDIENT	GRAMS	OUNCES	VOLUME	BAKER'S PERCENTAGE
Medium rye flour	400	14.10	3–3¼ cups	66.67%
Bread flour	200	7.05	1¼–1½ cups	33.33%
Warm (105°F/41°C) water	375	13.25	1½ cups + 2 Tbs.	62.50%
Salt	6	0.20	1 tsp.	1.00%
Instant yeast	5	0.20	1 Tbs.	0.83%
Sugar	5	0.20	1⅓ tsp.	0.83%
TOTAL FORMULA	998	35.20		165.17%
TOTAL FLOUR	600	21.15		100.00%
Rye flour for dusting	As needed			

recipe continues

1. Combine the dough ingredients in the mixer and use the dough hook at low (KA2) speed. The dough will quickly gather into a smooth, pliable mass that cleans the sides of the bowl, but continue kneading to develop the gluten, 8–10 minutes.

2. Turn the dough, which will be smooth, firm, and slightly tacky, onto a well-floured work surface. Divide it into two dozen 42 g/1½ oz. pieces and shape each into a ball the size of a golf ball. Flatten the dough balls by pressing them into the flour for dusting with the palm of your hand, then arrange them flour side up on parchment-lined baking sheet. Cover and proof at room temperature (68–72°F/20–22°C) until the surface of the dough shows cracking, 25–35 minutes.

3. Preheat the oven to 430°F/220°C with the baking surface in the upper third. Brush the rolls with water and bake until light golden brown, 18–22 minutes. Transfer to a rack and cool thoroughly.

Austrian Country Boule

Bauernlaib

AUSTRIA This spectacular bread from the Austrian-Bavarian border region show-cases rye's flavor in a smooth crumb made tender by stale rye bread. The loaf is huge—about 4 pounds/1.8 kg and 16 inches/40 cm in diameter—and it freezes beau-tifully. It's also visually striking: baking the bread seam-side up creates an appealing pattern of cracks in the top crust that stands in sharp contrast to its mantle of flour. The crumb is firm and open, the crust chewy, and the flavor brightly sour, perfumed with the sweet fragrance of fennel and the mild bite of caraway. Great with sausages, both fresh and cured—like the *soppressata* in the photograph—mild cheeses like Morbier, Comté, or Monterey Jack; or with nothing more than a light film of sweet butter.

RYE %:	**70%**
STAGES:	**Sponge, soaker, final dough**
LEAVEN:	**Rye sour culture, yeast**
START TO FINISH:	**24–26 hours**
HANDS-ON TIME:	**45–50 minutes**
YIELD:	**One 4 lb./1.8 kg loaf**

SPONGE (DAY 1, EVENING)

INGREDIENT	GRAMS	OUNCES	VOLUME	BAKER'S PERCENTAGE
White rye flour	280	9.90	2 cups	100%
Warm (105°F/41°C) water	220	7.75	1 cup	79%
Caraway seed	10	0.35	4½ tsp.	4%
Rye sour culture (see page 35)	10	0.35	2½ tsp.	4%

1. Combine the sponge ingredients, mix by hand into a stiff paste, and ferment at room temperature (68–72°F/20–22°C) place until bubbly and nearly collapsed, 15–20 hours. The sponge will have a very strong sour smell.

recipe continues

5. Flip the dough seam side up onto a well-floured peel, if using a baking stone, or onto a parchment-lined sheet pan. Cover and continue proofing until the boule shows a pattern of deep cracks and a finger pressed into the surface leaves a dent that doesn't spring back, 20–25 minutes.

6. Preheat the oven to 485°F/250°C with a steam pan (see page 76) and the baking surface in the middle. Bake with steam for 5 minutes, remove the steam pan, and bake for another 10 minutes. Lower the temperature to 385°F/200°C and bake until the loaf thumps when tapped with a finger and the internal temperature is at least 198°F/92°C, 80–90 minutes. Transfer to a rack and cool thoroughly before slicing.

BAKER'S PERCENTAGES

INGREDIENT	G	%
TOTAL FLOUR	1,000	100.00%
White rye flour	465	46.50%
Medium rye flour	235	23.50%
Bread flour	150	15.00%
Whole-wheat flour	150	15.00%
Water	670	67.00%
Salt	22	2.20%
Instant yeast	2	0.20%
Soaker water	100	10.00%
Stale bread	100	10.00%
Caraway seed	15	1.50%
Rye sour culture	10	1.00%
TOTAL FORMULA	1,919	191.90%
Total flour prefermented	280	28.00%

Caraway Beer Bread

Kümmel-Bier Brot

GERMANY This is a loaf that appeals to all my senses. Visually it's a stunning bread, with a glossy, deeply browned top crust. Its aroma carries the sharp edges of caraway and beer. The addition of stale rye bread tenderizes an even, pale tan crumb. The flavor profile is complex, combining the astringency of the caraway, understated sour of the sponge, and malty bite of *hefeweizen*, the pale wheat beer of southern Bavaria. Try it with sauerbraten or cold roast beef and English mustard.

RYE %:	**50%**
STAGES:	**Sponge, final dough**
LEAVEN:	**Rye sour culture**
START TO FINISH:	**16–20 hours**
HANDS-ON TIME:	**30–35 minutes**
YIELD:	**One 3½ lb./1.5 kg loaf or two 1¾ lb./750 g loaves**

SPONGE (DAY 1, EVENING)

INGREDIENT	GRAMS	OUNCES	VOLUME	BAKER'S PERCENTAGE
White rye flour	200	7.05	1⅜ cups	55%
Medium rye flour	165	5.80	1¼ cups	45%
Warm (105°F/41°C) water	300	10.60	1½ cups less 2 tsp.	82%
Rye sour culture (see page 35)	30	1.05	2½ Tbs.	8%

1. Mix the sponge ingredients by hand until incorporated, cover and ferment at room temperature (68–72°F/20–22°C) overnight, 12–15 hours. The sponge will be very bubbly, have a clean sour smell, and will have begun to fall back on itself.

recipe continues

Caraway Beer Bread is a traditional Bavarian pan bread that, true to its name, combines the sharp astringency of caraway seed with the malty bitterness of wheat beer (*hefeweizen*).

FINAL DOUGH (DAY 2, MORNING)

INGREDIENT	GRAMS	OUNCES	VOLUME
Sponge	695	24.50	Use all
Hefeweizen or other wheat beer, at room temperature	300	10.60	1¼ cups
First clear or high-gluten flour	500	17.65	3½ cups
White rye flour	135	4.75	
Salt	21	0.75	1¼ Tbs.
Malt syrup, light corn syrup, or light molasses	32	1.15	1½ Tbs.
Caraway seed	20	0.70	3 Tbs.
Flour for dusting	As needed		
Vegetable shortening for pans	As needed		
Beer for wash	As needed		

2. Combine the sponge, beer, and wheat flour in the mixer and use the paddle at low (KA2) speed to mix until blended, 2–3 minutes. Gradually add the rye flour, salt, syrup, and caraway seed and continue mixing until it forms a lumpy mass, 2–3 minutes. Switch to the dough hook and mix at low (KA2) speed until the dough is smooth and leaves the sides of the bowl, 6–8 minutes. Cover and ferment at room temperature until doubled in volume, 2–3 hours.

3. Turn the dough onto a lightly floured work surface and use floured hands to gently knead it back to its original size. Flatten into a square about 12-by-12 inches/30-by-30 cm and form a log by folding the far edge to the center and the new far edge to the near edge. Seal the seam with your fingertips and place the dough into a well-greased 13-by-4-by-4-inch/33-by-10-by-10 cm Pullman loaf pan or divide it in half and place it into two well-greased 8½-by-4½-by-2¾-inch/22-by-12-by-7 cm loaf pans. Slash the dough lengthwise to a depth of ¼–½ inch/0.6–1.25 cm, brush generously with beer, cover, and proof at room temperature until the dough reaches the top edge of the baking pan, 50–60 minutes.

recipe continues

4. Preheat the oven to maximum temperature, typically 500–550°F/260–290°C, with a steam pan (see page 76) and the baking surface in the middle. Brush the dough with beer, reduce the oven temperature to 465°F/240°C, and bake with steam for 25 minutes. Remove the steam pan and reduce the temperature to 340°F/170°C. Brush the top crust with beer once more, and bake until the loaf thumps when tapped with a finger and the internal temperature is at least 198°F/92°C, 40–45 minutes. Five minutes before baking is complete, brush the crust with beer and bake with the oven door ajar. Remove from the pans, transfer to a rack, and cool thoroughly before slicing.

BAKER'S PERCENTAGES

INGREDIENT	G	%
TOTAL FLOUR	1,000	100.00%
First clear flour	500	50.00%
White rye flour	335	33.50%
Medium rye flour	165	16.50%
Water	300	30.00%
Beer	300	30.00%
Salt	21	2.10%
Syrup	32	3.20%
Caraway seed	20	2.00%
Rye sour culture	30	3.00%
TOTAL FORMULA	1,703	170.30%
Total flour prefermented	365	36.50%

Valais Rye

Walliserbrot

SWITZERLAND Valais, in the High Alps, shares borders with France and Italy and is home to the Matterhorn and the winter sport mecca Zermatt. This variation on the canton's signature bread offers a firm, chewy crumb filled with the textural surprises of coarse rye meal, sunflower seeds, and a generous addition of walnuts. Rye dominates its flavor profile, with a well-balanced sour and subtly bitter finish that cuts through the richness of the nuts and seeds.

This bread pairs beautifully with tart fruit preserves or zesty cured meats or spread with Raclette, the region's best-known cheese, melted over an open flame.

RYE %:	**90%**
STAGES:	**Sponge, soaker, final dough**
LEAVEN:	**Rye sour culture, yeast**
START TO FINISH:	**15–20 hours**
HANDS-ON TIME:	**30–40 minutes**
YIELD:	**Two 2½ lb./1.15 kg loaves**

SPONGE (DAY 1, EVENING)

INGREDIENT	GRAMS	OUNCES	VOLUME	BAKER'S PERCENTAGE
Coarse rye meal	380	13.40	2½ cups	100%
Warm (105°F/41°C) water	306	10.80	1¼ cups	80%
Rye sour culture (see page 35)	39	1.35	3 Tbs.	10%

1. Mix the sponge ingredients by hand until incorporated, cover, and ferment at room temperature (68–72°F/20–22°C) overnight, 10–12 hours. The sponge will have a clean sour smell and will have barely expanded.

recipe continues

An abundance of plump, rich walnuts and fragrant sunflower seeds encased in a mildly sour rustic crumb are the hallmarks of Switzerland's **Valais Rye**, paired here with a ripe Gorgonzola.

SOAKER (DAY 1, EVENING)

INGREDIENT	GRAMS	OUNCES	VOLUME	BAKER'S PERCENTAGE
Sunflower seeds	56	1.95	⅜ cup	100%
Warm (105°F/41°C) water	56	1.95	¼ cup	100%
Salt	3	0.10	½ tsp.	5%

2. In a separate container, combine the soaker ingredients, cover, and let stand at room temperature overnight, 10–12 hours.

FINAL DOUGH (DAY 2, MORNING)

INGREDIENT	GRAMS	OUNCES	VOLUME
Sponge	725	25.55	Use all
Soaker	115	4.00	Use all
Medium rye flour	620	21.85	4.86 cup
Whole-wheat flour	111	3.90	1 cup less 1 Tbs.
Warm (105°F/41°C) water	639	22.55	2¾ cups
Salt	17	0.60	1 Tbs.
Instant yeast	7	0.25	1¾ tsp.
Walnuts, coarsely chopped	222	7.85	2 cups
Fine rye meal or medium rye flour for dusting	As needed		
Vegetable shortening for pan	As needed		

3. Combine the sponge, soaker, flours, warm water, salt, and yeast in the mixer and use the dough hook at low (KA2) speed to mix until developed into a very soft and very sticky dough, 10–12 minutes. Add the walnut pieces and mix until distributed evenly in the dough, 2–3 minutes. Cover the dough and ferment at room temperature until 1½ times its original volume, 75–90 minutes.

recipe continues

4. Turn the dough onto a work surface that has been generously dusted with fine rye meal or medium rye flour. Divide the dough into two pieces, each weighing about 1.2 kg/42 oz. Use a metal dough scraper and floured hands to shape each into an oblong, roll each piece in flour or rye meal to coat thoroughly, and place in a well-greased 9-by-4-by-4-inch/23-by-10-by-10 cm Pullman loaf pan or 9-by-5-by-3-inch/23-by-13-by-8 cm loaf pan. Cover and proof the loaves at room temperature until the dough reaches the rim of the pans and shows cracks or broken bubbles, 1–1½ hours.

5. Preheat the oven to the lower of 525°F/270°C or maximum temperature with a steam pan (see page 76) and the baking surface in the middle. Bake with steam for 10 minutes, then remove the steam pan, lower the temperature to 355°F/180°C, and bake until the loaf thumps when tapped with a finger and the internal temperature is at least 198°F/92°C, 70–80 minutes. Remove from the pans, transfer to a rack, and cool thoroughly before slicing.

BAKER'S PERCENTAGES

INGREDIENT	G	%
TOTAL FLOUR	1,111	100.00%
Medium rye flour	620	55.80%
Coarse rye meal	380	34.20%
Whole-wheat flour	111	10.00%
Water	945	85.06%
Salt	20	1.80%
Instant yeast	7	0.63%
Walnuts	222	19.98%
Soaker water	56	5.04%
Sunflower seeds	56	5.04%
Rye sour culture	39	3.51%
TOTAL FORMULA	2,456	221.06%
Total flour prefermented	380	34.20%

Franconia Crusty Boule

Fränkisches Krustenbrot

GERMANY This north Bavarian bread has a lot of moving parts—a three-stage rye sponge, a soaker, and a sour wheat sponge—and that's before you even get to the final dough. The result, however, is worth the effort. This is a rustic, full-flavored bread, with a dense, tender crumb and a thick, heavily cracked crust, the result of baking the bread seam side up in a very hot oven. The spices are optional but add yet another layer of flavor to the earthiness of the rye, the sweetness of the wheat, and the prominent, but not overwhelming, sour. This is a bread that goes beautifully with bratwurst and grilled onions, meat loaf, savory stews, and veined cheeses like Edelpilz and Bavarian blue (*Blauschimmelkäse*), accompanied by a Bavarian bock or lager beer.

RYE %:	**87%**
STAGES:	**3-stage rye sponge, wheat sponge, soaker, final dough**
LEAVEN:	**Rye sour culture**
START TO FINISH:	**26–28 hours**
HANDS-ON TIME:	**45–60 minutes**
YIELD:	**One 3½ lb./1.60 kg loaf**

STAGE 1 RYE SPONGE (DAY 1, MIDDAY)

INGREDIENT	GRAMS	OUNCES	VOLUME	BAKER'S PERCENTAGE
Medium rye flour	58	2.05	¼ cup	100%
Warm (105°F/41°C) water	58	2.05	2 Tbs.	100%
Rye sour culture (see page 35)	12	0.45	2½ tsp.	21%

1. Combine the Stage 1 ingredients, mix well, cover, and ferment at room temperature (68–72°F/20–22°C) for 8–10 hours. The sponge will have doubled in volume and have a clean sour smell.

recipe continues

STAGE 2 RYE SPONGE (DAY 1, EVENING)

INGREDIENT	GRAMS	OUNCES	VOLUME	BAKER'S PERCENTAGE
Medium rye flour	64	2.25	½ cup	100%
Warm (105°F/41°C) water	64	2.25	¼ cup	100%
Stage 1 sponge	128	4.50	Use all	200%

2. Add the Stage 2 ingredients to the Stage 1 sponge, mix well, cover, and ferment overnight, 8–10 hours. The sponge will be very bubbly and will have doubled in volume.

SOAKER (DAY 1, EVENING)

INGREDIENT	GRAMS	OUNCES	VOLUME	BAKER'S PERCENTAGE
Medium rye flour	250	8.80	2 cups	100%
Warm (105°F/41°C) water	200	7.05	⅞ cup	80%

3. In a separate container, combine the soaker ingredients, cover, and refrigerate until 2 hours before the final dough.

STAGE 3 RYE SPONGE (DAY 2, MORNING)

INGREDIENT	GRAMS	OUNCES	VOLUME	BAKER'S PERCENTAGE
Medium rye flour	128	4.50	1 cup	100%
Warm (105°F/41°C) water	128	4.50	½ cup	100%
Stage 2 sponge	256	9.00	Use all	200%

4. Add the Stage 3 ingredients to the Stage 2 sponge and ferment at room temperature until a small amount of sponge floats in water, 6–10 hours.

WHEAT SPONGE (DAY 2, MORNING)

INGREDIENT	GRAMS	OUNCES	VOLUME	BAKER'S PERCENTAGE
Whole-wheat flour	95	3.15	¾ cup	100%
Warm (105°F/41°C) water	95	3.15	⅜ cup	100%
Wheat or rye sour culture	10	0.70	1½ Tbs.	11%

5. In a separate container, combine the wheat sponge ingredients, cover, and let stand at room temperature until tripled in volume, 6–10 hours.

FINAL DOUGH (DAY 2, AFTERNOON)

INGREDIENT	GRAMS	OUNCES	VOLUME
Soaker	450	15.85	Use all
Stage 3 sponge	512	18.00	Use all
Wheat sponge	200	7.00	Use all
Medium rye flour	400	14.10	3 cups
Warm (105°F/41°C) water	150	5.30	⅝ cup
Salt	20	0.70	1 Tbs.
Bread spice (optional, page 43)	8	0.30	4 tsp.
Flour for dusting	As needed		

6. Combine the soaker, sponges, flour, warm water, salt, and bread spice, if desired, in the mixer. Mix at low (KA2) speed using the dough hook until evenly blended, 6–8 minutes. Cover the dough and ferment at room temperature until doubled, about 1 hour.

7. Turn the dough onto a well-floured work surface and use floured hands to flatten it into a disk, then pull the edges together, forming a ball, and seal. Put the dough seam side down into a well-floured bread form (see page 72) or cloth-lined basket, cover, and proof at room temperature until cracks appear in the dough, 60–75 minutes.

recipe continues

8. Preheat the oven to 520°F/270°C with a steam pan (see page 76) and the baking surface in the middle. Turn the dough seam side up onto a well-floured peel, if using a baking stone, or a parchment-lined sheet pan. Reduce the oven temperature to 485°F/250°C and bake with steam for 10 minutes, then remove the steam pan and reduce the temperature to 355°F/180°C. Bake until the loaf thumps when tapped with a finger and the internal temperature is at least 198°F/92°C, 60 65 minutes. Transfer to a rack and cool thoroughly before slicing.

BAKER'S PERCENTAGES

INGREDIENT	G	%
TOTAL FLOUR	995	100.00%
Medium rye flour	500	50.25%
Dark rye flour	400	40.20%
Whole-wheat flour	95	9.55%
Water	495	49.75%
Salt	20	2.01%
Soaker water	200	20.10%
Bread spice	8	0.80%
Rye sour culture	22	2.21%
TOTAL FORMULA	1,740	174.87%
Total flour prefermented	345	34.67%
Total rye flour prefermented	250	25.13%
Total wheat flour prefermented	95	9.55%

Like many Alpine breads, **Franconia Crusty Boule** uses multiple predoughs and the blend of spices called *brotgewürz* (see page 43) to produce a flavor profile that is as complex as it is appealing.

GOST Borodinsky. If Russia has a national bread, it's Borodinsky (shown here with hot-smoked lake trout), a dark, open-crumbed, intensely sour bread that embodies the forceful personality of its native land.

1. Mix the sponge ingredients by hand until incorporated, cover, and ferment at room temperature (68–72°F/20–22°C) for 10–12 hours, preferably overnight. The sponge will be very bubbly, have a clean sour smell, and will have doubled in volume.

SCALD (DAY 1, EVENING)

INGREDIENT	GRAMS	OUNCES	VOLUME	BAKER'S PERCENTAGE
Coarse rye meal	115	4.05	¾ cup	100%
Red rye malt (see page 42)	35	1.25	¼ cup	30%
Boiling water	300	10.60	1¼ cups	261%
Ground coriander	4	0.15	1 Tbs.	3%

2. Mix the scald ingredients by hand, cover, and let stand for 8–10 hours or overnight.

SCALD-SPONGE (DAY 2, MORNING)

INGREDIENT	GRAMS	OUNCES	VOLUME	BAKER'S PERCENTAGE
Sponge	725	25.55	Use all	100%
Scald	454	16.00	Use all	63%

3. Combine the sponge and scald in the mixer, cover, and ferment at room temperature until doubled in bulk, 3–4 hours.

FINAL DOUGH (DAY 2, AFTERNOON)

INGREDIENT	GRAMS	OUNCES	VOLUME
Scald-sponge	1,179	41.55	Use all
Medium rye flour	210	7.40	1⅔ cups
Bread flour	140	4.95	1 cup
Salt	10	0.35	1⅔ tsp
Unsulphured dark molasses	40	1.40	2 Tbs.
Red rye malt (see page 42)	10	0.35	1 Tbs.
Vegetable shortening for pan	As needed		
Coriander seed	2	0.05	1–2 tsp.

recipe continues

4. Add the flours, salt, molasses, and red rye malt to the scald-sponge and use the dough hook at low (KA2) speed to mix to a soft, smooth, deep brown dough, 8–10 minutes. Cover and ferment at room temperature until visibly expanded, 60–75 minutes.

5. Carefully spoon the dough into a well-greased 9-by-4-by-4-inch/23-by-10-by-10 cm Pullman loaf pan. Use wet hands to distribute the dough evenly and smooth the top. Spoon 15 ml/0.5 oz./1 Tbs. of water over the loaf to keep the dough moist, then cover and proof at room temperature until the top of the loaf shows broken bubbles, 1½–2 hours. Brush with water and garnish with whole or coarsely crushed coriander seed.

6. Preheat the oven to 550°F/290°C with a steam pan (see page 76) and the baking surface in the middle. Bake with steam for 10 minutes. Remove the steam pan, cover the loaf with aluminum foil, and reduce the temperature to 350°F/175°C. Bake for 45–50 minutes, then remove the loaf and return it to the oven to firm the side and bottom crusts. Bake until the loaf thumps when tapped with a finger and the internal temperature is at least 198°F/92°C, 10–15 minutes. Transfer to a rack and cool thoroughly before slicing.

BAKER'S PERCENTAGES

INGREDIENT	G	%
TOTAL FLOUR	730	100.00%
Medium rye flour	475	65.07%
Bread flour	140	19.18%
Coarse rye meal	115	15.75%
Water	730	100.00%
Salt	10	1.37%
Red rye malt	45	6.16%
Molasses	40	5.48%
Coriander	4	0.55%
Rye sour culture	30	4.11%
TOTAL FORMULA	1,589	217.67%
Total flour prefermented	380	28.40%

Christmas Bread

Kaledu Pyragas

LITHUANIA We took this bread to a neighborhood holiday party, unsure of the reception it would get; it disappeared very quickly. This is a typically sweet-sour Baltic rye bread—close and tender crumbed, with a clean, assertively sour flavor profile. But there's more: in honor of Jesus's birth, the Lithuanians add honey, raisins, dried apricots, and prunes—commonplace today, but rare out-of-season luxuries not so long ago—to this everyday bread. The fruit and honey add both sweetness and their distinctively nuanced acid notes to the loaf, creating a complex interplay of sugar, citric acid, and lactic acid. This loaf also offers the textural and visual contrasts of tender orange apricots and dark brown prunes and raisins against the firm pale-tan crumb. Eat it buttered or plain—I like it toasted—with a strong-flavored cheese and a glass of sweet wine.

RYE %:	**100%**
STAGES:	**2-stage sponge, final dough**
LEAVEN:	**Rye sour culture**
START TO FINISH:	**20–24 hours**
HANDS-ON TIME:	**35–40 minutes**
YIELD:	**One 2¾ lb./1.25 kg loaf**

STAGE 1 SPONGE (DAY 1, MIDDAY)

INGREDIENT	GRAMS	OUNCES	VOLUME	BAKER'S PERCENTAGE
Medium rye flour	115	4.05	⅞ cup	100%
Warm (105°F/41°C) water	95	3.35	⅜ cup	83%
Rye sour culture (see page 35)	10	0.35	2½ tsp.	9%

1. Mix the sponge ingredients by hand until incorporated, cover and ferment at room temperature (68–72°F/20–22°C) overnight, 10–12 hours. The sponge will be very bubbly, have a clean sour smell, and will have doubled in volume.

recipe continues

In the Baltics, as elsewhere in Europe, the common folk marked special occasions by adding sweet delicacies to their daily bread. **Lithuanian Christmas Bread** is a perfect example, offsetting the robust, sour crumb with raisins, dried fruit, and honey.

STAGE 2 SPONGE (DAY 1, EVENING)

INGREDIENT	GRAMS	OUNCES	VOLUME	BAKER'S PERCENTAGE
White rye flour	130	4.60	1 cup less 1 Tbs.	100%
Warm (105°F/41°C) water	150	5.30	⅝ cup	115%
Stage 1 sponge	220	7.75	Use all	168%

2. Add the flour and warm water to the Stage 1 sponge, mix to incorporate, cover, and ferment at room temperature overnight, 8–10 hours. The sponge will be bubbly, have an intense sour smell, and will have tripled in volume

FINAL DOUGH (DAY 2, MORNING)

INGREDIENT	GRAMS	OUNCES	VOLUME
White rye flour	250	8.80	1¾ cups
Warm (105°F/41°C) water	100	3.55	⅜ cup + 1 Tbs.
Salt	10	0.35	1⅔ tsp.
Honey, preferably dark	40	1.40	2 Tbs.
Red rye malt (see page 42)	10	0.35	1 Tbs.
Stage 2 sponge	500	17.65	Use all
Pitted prunes, quartered	100	3.55	⅝ cup
Dried unsulphured apricots, quartered	75	2.65	⅝ cup
Raisins	50	1.75	⅓ cup
Vegetable shortening for pan	As needed		

3. Combine the flour, warm water, salt, honey, red rye malt, and Stage 2 sponge in the mixer and use the dough hook at low (KA2) speed, scraping down the bowl as necessary, until the dough becomes a sticky, stringy mass, 5–6 minutes. Add the dried fruit and continue mixing until the fruit is well distributed, 2–3 minutes.

recipe continues

4. Use a plastic scraper to transfer the dough to a well-greased 9-by-4-by-4-inch/23-by-10-by-10 cm Pullman loaf pan or 9-by-5-by-3-inch/23-by-13-by-8 cm standard loaf pan. Use wet hands to smooth the dough, which will half fill the pan. Cover with plastic wrap and proof in an oven that's been preheated to 100°F/38°C and turned off until the dough reaches the rim of the pan, 1–3 hours.

5. Remove the dough from the oven and preheat to 430°F/220°C with a steam pan (see page 76) and the baking surface in the middle. Bake with steam for 10 minutes, then remove the steam pan. Lower the oven temperature to 365°F/185°C and continue baking until the loaf thumps when tapped with a finger and the internal temperature is at least 198°F/92°C, 30–40 minutes. Remove the loaf from the pan, transfer to a rack, and cool thoroughly before slicing.

BAKER'S PERCENTAGES

INGREDIENT	G	%
TOTAL FLOUR	495	100.00%
White rye flour	380	76.77%
Medium rye flour	115	23.23%
Water	345	69.70%
Salt	10	2.02%
Prunes	100	20.20%
Dried apricots	75	15.15%
Raisins	50	10.10%
Honey	40	8.08%
Red rye malt	10	2.02%
Rye sour culture	10	2.02%
TOTAL FORMULA	1,135	229.29%
Total flour prefermented	245	49.49%

Riga Rye

Rudzu Maize

`LATVIA` Of all the breads of Eastern Europe, the breads of Latvia are held in highest regard, and no wonder. This extraordinary 4-pound loaf is a classic from a region that likes its breads big—sometimes as big as 9 lb./4 kg.

Its flavor is lush—in stark contrast to the austerity of its ingredients. The rye's nuttiness is set off by the musky, slightly bitter sweetness of molasses, malted rye, and the sugars released during the scald. Beneath that sweetness lurks a clean unobtrusive sour that plays against a caraway edge. The crust is beautifully shiny and smooth—in that part of the world torn crusts signify an inexperienced baker—and the crumb is dense and very tender. It goes with everything, from honey and preserves to tart salads and savory meats and cheeses; but this bread is so good that, to me, even a light film of butter is a distraction.

RYE %:	**89%**
STAGES:	**Sponge, scald, scald-sponge, final dough**
LEAVEN:	**Rye sour culture, yeast**
START TO FINISH:	**12–16 hours**
HANDS-ON TIME:	**45–60 minutes**
YIELD:	**One 4½ lb./2.05 kg loaf**

SPONGE (DAY 1, MORNING)

INGREDIENT	GRAMS	OUNCES	VOLUME	BAKER'S PERCENTAGE
Medium rye flour	70	2.45	½ cup	100%
Warm (105°F/41°C) water	30	1.05	2 Tbs.	43%
Rye sour culture (see page 35)	100	3.55	½ cup	143%

1. Mix the sponge ingredients by hand until incorporated into a very stiff dough, cover and ferment at room temperature (68–72°F/20–22°C) for 3½–4 hours. The sponge will have a clean sour smell and will have doubled in volume.

recipe continues

SCALD (DAY 1, MORNING)

INGREDIENT	GRAMS	OUNCES	VOLUME	BAKER'S PERCENTAGE
Medium rye flour	350	12.35	2¾ cups	100%
Boiling water	560	19.75	2⅜ cups	160%
Caraway seed	6	0.20	2½ tsp.	2%
Malted rye	70	2.45	½ cup	20%

2. In a separate container, mix the flour, boiling water, and caraway seed by hand into a stiff paste and let stand for 4–5 minutes. Use a blender or spice grinder to grind the malted rye into a fine powder, then stir it into the scald. Cover and place in a warm (145–150°F/63–65°C) oven for 3 hours. If the oven's lowest temperature is above this range, preheat to its minimum temperature and turn the oven off. Check the oven thermometer every 45–60 minutes and reheat as necessary. During that time the scald will loosen considerably and become very sweet and fragrant.

SCALD-SPONGE (DAY 1, MIDDAY)

INGREDIENT	GRAMS	OUNCES	VOLUME	BAKER'S PERCENTAGE
Sponge	200	7.05	Use all	20%
Scald	986	34.75	Use all	100%
White rye flour	70	2.45	½ cup	7%
Instant yeast	2	0.05	⅓ tsp.	0.2%

3. Combine the sponge, scald, flour, and yeast in the mixer and mix by hand until blended. Preheat the oven to 100°F/38°C (check the oven thermometer), then turn it off. Cover the scald-sponge and ferment in the oven, reheating to 100°F/38°C hourly, until doubled in bulk and fragrant with the smell of sour apples, 3–5 hours. The longer the ferment, the stronger the smell.

FINAL DOUGH (DAY 1, AFTERNOON)

INGREDIENT	GRAMS	OUNCES	VOLUME
Unsulphured dark molasses	70	2.45	¼ cup less 2 tsp.
Water	170	6.00	¾ cup
White rye flour	658	23.20	4⅔ cups
AP flour	140	4.95	1 cup
Salt	30	1.05	5 tsp.
Scald-sponge	1,258	44.30	Use all

4. Dissolve the molasses in the water and add it, along with the flours and salt, to the scald-sponge. Use the dough hook and mix at low (KA2) speed until the dough comes together in a stiff mass and starts gathering around the hook, 7–8 minutes. Cover and ferment in the warm oven, reheating to 100°F/38°C hourly, until doubled in bulk, 2–3 hours.

5. Turn the dough onto a sheet of parchment paper and use wet hands to shape it into a rounded oblong. Proof it in the warmed oven until doubled, 75–80 minutes, using wet hands to smooth the broken bubbles out of the crust after 35 minutes and again when proofing is complete.

6. Preheat the oven to 535°F/280°C with a steam pan (see page 76) and the baking surface in the upper third. Use a chopstick or skewer to dock the loaf three times to its full depth and brush the crust with water. Bake with steam for 12 minutes, then remove the steam pan, lower the temperature to 410°F/210°C, and bake until the loaf thumps when tapped with a finger and the internal temperature is at least 198°F/92°C, 40–45 minutes.

GLAZE

INGREDIENT	GRAMS	OUNCES	VOLUME	BAKER'S PERCENTAGE
Cornstarch or potato starch	3	0.10	1 tsp.	100%
Water	227	8.00	1 cup	250%

recipe continues

7. While the bread is baking, dissolve the starch in 28 ml/1.00 oz./2 Tbs. of the water and bring the remaining water to a boil. Stir the starch mixture (it will settle) and pour it into the boiling water, stirring constantly until the glaze thickens to the consistency of honey, 3–4 minutes. Remove from the heat and let cool to room temperature.

8. Five minutes before baking is complete, glaze the loaf. Transfer to a rack and cool for 10–12 hours before slicing.

BAKER'S PERCENTAGES

INGREDIENT	G	%
TOTAL FLOUR	1,288	100.00%
White rye flour	728	56.52%
Medium rye flour	420	32.61%
AP flour	140	10.87%
Water	760	59.01%
Salt	30	2.33%
Instant yeast	2	0.16%
Malted rye	70	5.43%
Molasses	70	5.43%
Caraway seed	6	0.47%
TOTAL FORMULA	2,226	172.83%
Total flour prefermented	490	38.04%

The Latvians are considered Eastern Europe's finest bakers, and with good reason. This big (4 lb./2 kg) **Riga Rye,** shown here with cold-smoked Pacific saury (a mackerel-like fish), uses a scald (see page 58) to liberate rye's abundant natural sugars.

Minsk Rye , paired here with a traditional topping of Russian butter, radishes, and salt, is built on a dough that's 90% white rye flour, which distinguishes it from the darker, more strongly flavored breads of northern Russia and the Baltics. Its dense crumb and lush flavors make me think of it as New York Corn Rye (page 87) on steroids.

Minsk Rye

Chleb Minskiy

BELARUS This bread is a rarity among the northern ryes of Eastern Europe—not because of its high percentage of rye flour, 90%, but because that rye flour is all white in a bread that comes from Belarus, well north of white rye country.

The dough is very easy to work. Its dominant taste is caraway-edged with sweetness and a sour finish that builds through the chew. Its light brown crumb is dense, moist, and tender; its flavor and mouthfeel take me back to the brawny New York Corn Rye (page 87) I ate as a kid, only better. Anywhere a New York rye goes, so does this one—with corned beef, tongue, and pastrami. In this bread, the New York classic may have finally met its match.

RYE %:	**90%**
STAGES:	**Sponge, final dough**
LEAVEN:	**Rye sour culture, yeast**
START TO FINISH:	**18–20 hours**
HANDS-ON TIME:	**20–30 minutes**
YIELD:	**Two 1¾ lb./800 g loaves or one 3½ lb./1.60 kg loaf**

SPONGE (DAY 1, EVENING)

INGREDIENT	GRAMS	OUNCES	VOLUME	BAKER'S PERCENTAGE
White rye flour	311	10.95	2¼ cups	100%
Warm (105°F/41°C) water	249	8.80	1 cup + 1 Tbs.	80%
Rye sour culture (see page 35)	30	1.05	2½ Tbs.	10%

1. Mix the sponge ingredients by hand until incorporated, cover, and ferment at room temperature (68–72°F/20–22°C) overnight, 10–12 hours. The sponge will be very bubbly, have a clean sour smell, and will have doubled in volume.

recipe continues

FINAL DOUGH (DAY 2, MORNING)

INGREDIENT	GRAMS	OUNCES	VOLUME
Sponge	590	20.80	Use all
White rye flour	600	21.15	4¼ cups
Bread flour	100	3.55	¾ cup
Warm (105°F/41°C) water	410	14.45	1¾ cups
Salt	15	0.55	2½ tsp.
Instant yeast	2	0.05	½ tsp.
Malt powder	20	0.70	2 Tbs.
Unsulphured dark molasses	20	0.70	1 Tbs.
Caraway seed	2	0.05	1 tsp.
White rye flour for dusting	As needed		

2. Combine the sponge and final dough ingredients in the mixer and use the dough hook at low (KA2) speed to mix until smooth and fully developed, 6–8 minutes. Cover and ferment at room temperature until the dough has nearly doubled, 60–75 minutes.

3. Turn the dough, which will be soft and moderately sticky, onto a well-floured work surface and use floured hands to knead it back to its original volume. Divide the dough into two pieces, each weighing approximately 850 g/ 30 oz. or leave it whole. Shape the dough into a rounded oblong and place on a well-floured peel, if using a baking stone, or a parchment-lined baking sheet. Cover and proof at room temperature until the loaf has increased to 1½ times its original size and cracks or broken bubbles appear on the surface of the dough, 30–35 minutes.

4. Preheat the oven to 485°F/250°C with a steam pan (see page 76) and the baking surface in the middle. Bake with steam for 10 minutes, then remove the steam pan, reduce the temperature to 350°F/175°C, and bake until the loaf thumps when tapped with a finger and the internal temperature is at least 198°F/92°C, 60–75 minutes. Transfer to a rack and cool thoroughly before slicing.

BAKER'S PERCENTAGES

INGREDIENT	G	%
TOTAL FLOUR	1,011	100.00%
White rye flour	911	90.11%
Bread flour	100	9.89%
Water	659	65.18%
Salt	15	1.48%
Instant yeast	2	0.20%
Malt powder	20	1.98%
Molasses	20	1.98%
Caraway seed	2	0.20%
TOTAL FORMULA	1,729	171.02%
Total flour prefermented	311	30.76%

Vilnius Rye Bread

Ruginė Duona Vilniuje

LITHUANIA There's lots going on in this Vilnius-style rye. It's a simple recipe that produces a soft, sticky, unruly dough. The end product justifies the effort, however. Plum jam and rye malt add a balancing sweetness to the acidity of its two-stage sponge. Cumin contributes a spicy edge. Its close, coffee-brown crumb has an almost cakelike softness. Eat it with herring and beet salad or sour cream garnished with chopped cucumbers and radishes.

RYE %:	**100%**
STAGES:	**2-stage sponge, final dough**
LEAVEN:	**Rye sour culture**
START TO FINISH:	**16–23 hours**
HANDS-ON TIME:	**45–60 minutes**
YIELD:	**Two 1¾ lb./800 g loaves**

STAGE 1 SPONGE (DAY 1, EVENING)

INGREDIENT	GRAMS	OUNCES	VOLUME	BAKER'S PERCENTAGE
Medium rye flour	235	8.30	1⅚ cups	100%
Warm (105°F/41°C) water	190	6.70	¾ cup + 4 tsp.	81%
Rye sour culture (see page 35)	25	0.90	2 Tbs.	11%

1. Mix the Stage 1 ingredients by hand until incorporated, cover and ferment at room temperature (68–72°F/20–22°C) for 10–12 hours or overnight. The sponge will be very bubbly, have a clean sour smell, and will have doubled in volume.

STAGE 2 SPONGE (DAY 2, MORNING)

INGREDIENT	GRAMS	OUNCES	VOLUME	BAKER'S PERCENTAGE
Medium rye flour	250	8.80	2 cups	100%
Warm (105°F/41°C) water	250	8.80	1 cup + 5 tsp.	100%
Stage 1 sponge	450	15.90	Use all	180%

2. Add the Stage 2 ingredients to the Stage 1 sponge, mix by hand to incorporate, cover, and ferment at room temperature until it doubles in volume and becomes very bubbly, 6–8 hours.

FINAL DOUGH (DAY 2, AFTERNOON)

INGREDIENT	GRAMS	OUNCES	VOLUME
Red rye malt (see page 42)	20	0.71	2 Tbs.
Stage 2 sponge	950	33.50	Use all
Warm (105°F/41°C) water	350	12.35	1½ cups
Plum jam	60	2.12	3 Tbs.
Medium rye flour	200	7.05	1½ cups
White rye flour	160	5.64	1⅛ cups
Salt	20	0.71	3¼ tsp.
Ground cumin seed	10	0.35	5 tsp.
Vegetable shortening for pan	As needed		

3. Combine the red rye malt, Stage 2 sponge, warm water, and plum jam in the mixer and use the paddle at low (KA2) speed to mix until evenly blended, 4–6 minutes, then add the flours, salt and ground cumin and continue mixing into a soft dough, 6–8 minutes.

4. Place about 850 g/30 oz. of the dough into two well-greased 8½-by-4½-by-2¾-inch/22-by-12-by-7 cm loaf pans and use wet hands to smooth the top surfaces. Cover and proof at room temperature until the dough comes within 1 inch/2.5 cm of the rim of the loaf pans, 1–2 hours.

recipe continues

5. Preheat the oven to 445°F/230°C with a steam pan (see page 76) and the baking surface in the middle. Bake with steam for 5 minutes, then remove the steam pan, lower the oven temperature to 375°F/190°C, and bake until the loaf thumps when tapped with a finger and the internal temperature is at least 198°F/92°C, 40–45 minutes. Remove from the pans, transfer to a rack, spray the crust with water, and cool thoroughly before slicing.

BAKER'S PERCENTAGES

INGREDIENT	G	%
TOTAL FLOUR	845	100.00%
Medium rye flour	685	81.07%
White rye flour	160	18.93%
Water	790	93.49%
Salt	20	2.37%
Plum jam	60	7.10%
Red rye malt	20	2.37%
Cumin seed	10	1.18%
Rye sour culture	25	2.96%
TOTAL FORMULA	1,770	209.47%
Total flour prefermented	485	57.40%

Raisin-Orange Rye

Morskoy Chleb

RUSSIA In the days when Russians had limited access to nonlocal ingredients, they marked special occasions with sweet additions to their daily bread. This is a basic sour rye, baked round in the Russian style and enriched with milk, raisins, orange peel, both candied and raw, and a hint of honey. Compared with other Russian rye breads, its preparation is straightforward, using only two sponges and a final dough.

This bread is rich in flavor. The muted bitterness of the orange zest complements the nuttiness of the rye and cuts through the sweetness of the raisins and candied orange peel. The crumb is close and tender, studded with soft, sweet raisins, and chewy nuggets of orange peel—in all, an engaging chew. This is a perfect breakfast or afternoon snack bread that wants nothing more than a light film of butter or cream cheese and a cup of coffee or tea.

RYE %:	**100%**
STAGES:	**Sour sponge, milk sponge, final dough**
LEAVEN:	**Rye sour culture, yeast**
START TO FINISH:	**20–23 hours**
HANDS-ON TIME:	**30–40 minutes**
YIELD:	**One 2¼ lb./1.05 kg loaf**

SOUR SPONGE (DAY 1, EVENING)

INGREDIENT	GRAMS	OUNCES	VOLUME	BAKER'S PERCENTAGE
Medium rye flour	50	1.75	½ cup less 2 Tbs.	100%
Warm (105°F/41°C) water	35	1.25	2 Tbs. + ¾ tsp.	70%
Rye sour culture (see page 35)	9	0.30	2 tsp.	17%

1. Mix the sponge ingredients by hand until incorporated, cover, and ferment at room temperature (68–72°F/20–22°C) overnight, 10–12 hours. The sponge will be very bubbly, have a clean sour smell, and will have doubled in volume.

recipe continues

A heavy coating of honey glaze and a dense, crumbly crumb perfumed with orange zest, candied orange peel, and raisins makes **Raisin-Orange Rye**, enjoyed here with a glass of tea, as much a cake as it is a bread.

MILK SPONGE (DAY 2, MORNING)

INGREDIENT	GRAMS	OUNCES	VOLUME	BAKER'S PERCENTAGE
Whole milk, warmed to 105°F/41°C	275	9.70	1 cup + 2 Tbs.	125%
Sour Sponge	94	3.30	Use all	43%
Medium rye flour	220	7.75	1¾ cups	100%
Instant yeast	2	0.10	½ tsp.	1%

2. In a saucepan, bring the milk to a boil and let cool to lukewarm (85°F/30°C). Dissolve the sour sponge in the warm milk and add it to the flour and yeast in the mixer bowl. Mix by hand until lump-free, cover, and ferment at room temperature until doubled in volume, 4–5 hours.

FINAL DOUGH (DAY 2, AFTERNOON)

INGREDIENT	GRAMS	OUNCES	VOLUME
Warm (105°F/41°C) water	121	4.25	½ cup
Honey or light corn syrup	21	0.75	1 Tbs.
Milk sponge	591	20.80	Use all
White rye flour	275	9.70	2 cups less 1 Tbs.
Salt	10	0.35	1½ tsp.
Raisins	110	3.90	¾ cup
Candied orange peel	28	1.00	2 Tbs.
Grated zest of 1 ½–2 oranges	10	0.35	4 tsp.
Vegetable shortening for pan	As needed		

3. Add the warm water and honey to the milk sponge and mix by hand until evenly blended. Add the flour and salt and use the dough hook at low (KA2) speed to mix into a loose, lump-free dough, 5–6 minutes. Add the raisins, candied peel, and orange zest and mix to blend, 1–2 minutes. Cover and ferment at room temperature until nearly tripled in volume, 1½–2 hours.

recipe continues

4. Use wet hands to lightly knead the dough in the bowl back to its original volume, then transfer it directly to a well-greased 8-inch/20 cm Dutch oven, charlotte mold, or 8-by-3-inch/20-by-8 cm round cake pan. Use wet hands to smooth the top, cover, and proof at room temperature until the dough reaches the top of the pan and the surface shows broken bubbles, 60–75 minutes.

GLAZE

INGREDIENT	GRAMS	OUNCES	VOLUME
Light corn syrup or honey	21	0.75	1 Tbs.
Warm (105°F/41°C) water	14	0.50	1 Tbs.

5. Preheat the oven to 430°F/220°C with the baking surface in the middle. Combine the glaze ingredients and brush the loaf generously with the mixture. Bake for 10 minutes, then lower the temperature to 390°F/200°C and bake until the loaf thumps when tapped with a finger and the internal temperature is at least 198°F/92°C, 50–55 minutes. Remove from the pan, transfer to a rack, brush again with the glaze, and let stand for 12–24 hours before slicing.

BAKER'S PERCENTAGES

INGREDIENT	G	%
TOTAL FLOUR	545	100.00%
White rye flour	275	50.46%
Medium rye flour	270	49.54%
Milk	275	50.46%
Water	156	28.62%
Salt	10	1.74%
Instant yeast	2	0.28%
Raisins	110	20.18%
Candied orange peel	28	5.23%
Syrup	21	3.85%
Rye sour	9	1.56%
Orange zest	10	1.38%
TOTAL FORMULA	1,166	213.30%
Total flour prefermented	270	49.54%

Belarusian Sweet Rye

Chleb Yubilyarniy

BELARUS No other recipe I've encountered illustrates more vividly the creativity of Europe's rye bakers. The bread comes together in five stages—two scalds, two scald-sponges, and a final dough. Each stage builds on the previous one, using rye's chemistry to wring the last iota of flavor from a limited list of ingredients. Rye malt imparts a slightly burnt sweetness, while potato contributes tenderness to the dense, close crumb. The two scalds—one using rye and the other boiled potato— both include rye and barley malt, which contribute the enzymes that transform their starches into sugar. The crumb is dark brown and firm, the flavor reminiscent of a chocolate malted with a delicate sour finish. The subtlety of its flavor profile makes this bread a perfect foil for intensely flavored dry sausages like *soppressata*, Polish *swojska*, and German *landjäger* and pungent washed-rind cheeses such as Taleggio, ripe Camembert, and my own favorite, stinky Limburger topped with a shaving of raw onion.

RYE %:	**94%**
STAGES:	**Rye scald, scald-sponge, potato scald, *opara* sponge, final dough**
LEAVEN:	**Rye sour culture, yeast**
START TO FINISH:	**20–22 hours**
HANDS-ON TIME:	**40–50 minutes**
YIELD:	**Two 1¾ lb./800 g loaves**

RYE SCALD (DAY 1, EVENING)

INGREDIENT	GRAMS	OUNCES	VOLUME	BAKER'S PERCENTAGE
Medium rye flour	140	4.95	1 cup + 2 Tbs.	100%
Hot (150°F/65°C) water	350	12.35	1½ cups	250%
Red rye malt (see page 42)	60	2.10	⅜ cup	43%
Diastatic malt powder	20	0.70	2 Tbs.	14%

1. Mix the rye scald ingredients by hand, cover, and let stand at room temperature (68–72°F/20–22°C) for 1½–2 hours. The scald will have a strong chocolate malted color and smell.

recipe continues

SCALD-SPONGE (DAY 1, LATE EVENING)

INGREDIENT	GRAMS	OUNCES	VOLUME	BAKER'S PERCENTAGE
Rye scald	570	20.10	Use all	100%
Rye sour culture (see page 35)	80	2.80	⅜ cup	14%

2. Mix the rye scaled and rye sour culture by hand until incorporated, cover, and ferment at room temperature overnight, 10–12 hours. The sponge will be very bubbly, have a clean sour smell, and will have doubled in volume.

POTATO SCALD (DAY 2, EARLY MORNING)

INGREDIENT	GRAMS	OUNCES	VOLUME	BAKER'S PERCENTAGE
Boiled potato, riced	210	7.40	1 cup	100%
Hot (150°F/65°C) water	100	3.55	½ cup less 1 Tbs.	48%
Red rye malt (see page 42)	20	0.70	2 Tbs.	10%
Diastatic malt powder	10	0.35	1 Tbs.	5%

3. Mix the potato scald ingredients by hand, cover and let stand at room temperature for 2–4 hours.

OPARA SPONGE (DAY 2, MORNING)

INGREDIENT	GRAMS	OUNCES	VOLUME	BAKER'S PERCENTAGE
Scald-sponge	650	22.95	Use all	100%
Potato scald	340	12.00	Use all	52%
Whole-wheat flour	50	1.75	⅜ cup	8%
Warm (105°F/41°C) water	50	1.75	¼ cup less 1½ tsp.	8%
Instant yeast	2	0.05	⅓ tsp.	0.3%

4. Mix the *opara* sponge ingredients by hand until incorporated, cover, and ferment at room temperature for 2–3 hours. The sponge will show bubbles on the surface and will have visibly expanded.

FINAL DOUGH (DAY 2, AFTERNOON)

INGREDIENT	GRAMS	OUNCES	VOLUME
Opara sponge	1,092	38.50	Use all
Medium rye flour	682	24.05	5⅓ cups
Salt	15	0.55	2½ tsp.
Instant yeast	4	0.15	1⅓ tsp.
Honey	30	1.05	4¼ tsp.
Medium rye flour for dusting	As needed		

5. Combine the final dough ingredients in the bowl of the mixer and use the dough hook at low (KA2) speed to mix until the dough cleans the sides of the bowl and gathers around the hook, 6–8 minutes. Cover and ferment at room temperature until the dough has doubled in volume, 1–1½ hours.

6. Turn the dough onto a lightly floured work surface and use floured hands to knead the dough back to its original volume. It will be firm and slightly sticky but very easy to work. Divide the dough into two pieces, each weighing about 870 g/31 oz. and shape them into rounded oblongs about 12 inches/30 cm long and 4 inches/10 cm wide. Place on a well-floured peel, if using a baking stone, or a parchment-lined baking sheet. Cover with a damp cloth and proof at room temperature until the loaves have expanded to 1½ times their original volume and the surface shows broken bubbles, 25–35 minutes.

7. Preheat the oven to 410°F/210°C with the baking surface in the middle. Use a docking wheel, chopstick, or skewer to dock the top surface evenly to a depth of at least ¼ inch/0.6 cm and bake until the loaves thump when tapped with a finger and the internal temperature is at least 198°F/92°C, 45–50 minutes. Five minutes before the end of baking, brush or spray the crust with water. Transfer to a rack and cool thoroughly before slicing.

recipe continues

BAKER'S PERCENTAGES

INGREDIENT	G	%
TOTAL FLOUR	872	100.00%
Medium rye flour	822	94.27%
Whole-wheat flour	50	5.73%
Water	500	57.34%
Salt	15	1.72%
Instant yeast	6	0.69%
Boiled potato	210	24.08%
Red rye malt	80	9.17%
Honey	30	3.44%
Malt powder	30	3.44%
TOTAL FORMULA	1,743	199.88%
Total flour prefermented	190	21.79%

Spiced Honey Squares

Ruginė Riekelė

`LITHUANIA` This quick and easy bite has more in common with sweet Scandinavian breads than it does with the complex sweet-sour breads of the Baltics—and that's part of its charm. Like the spiced sweet breads of Sweden and southern Finland, it's aromatic with cumin and built on a yeast-leavened dough. The honey brings a subtly acidic sweetness that plays nicely against the nutty spiciness of the rye. The crumb is open and tender, the color a warm caramel brown. Eat these with cream cheese, homemade preserves, or butter for a satisfying breakfast, lunch, or snack.

RYE %:	**100%**
STAGES:	**Straight dough**
LEAVEN:	**Yeast**
START TO FINISH:	**2½ hours**
HANDS-ON TIME:	**30 minutes**
YIELD:	**One dozen 2¾ oz./80 g squares**

INGREDIENT	GRAMS	OUNCES	VOLUME	BAKER'S PERCENTAGE
Honey, preferably dark	70	2.45	¼ cup	14.00%
Instant yeast	7	0.25	1¾ tsp.	1.40%
Warm (105°F/41°C) water, or more as needed	375	13.20	1⅔ cups	75.00%
Medium rye flour	500	17.65	4 cups	100.00%
Salt	12	0.40	2 tsp.	2.40%
Cumin or fennel seed	4	0.15	2 tsp .	0.80%
TOTAL FORMULA	979	34.10		196.60%
Flour for dusting	As needed			

1. In the bowl of a mixer, dissolve the honey and yeast in the warm water and then add the flour, salt, and cumin. Use the dough hook at low (KA2) speed to mix until evenly blended into a fairly stiff but pliable dough, 5–6 minutes, adding more water, 15 ml/0.5 oz./1 Tbs. at a time, if needed. Cover and ferment at room temperature, 68–72°F/20–22°C, until the dough has visibly expanded, 60–75 minutes.

recipe continues

FINAL DOUGH (DAY 2, MORNING)

INGREDIENT	GRAMS	OUNCES	VOLUME
Sponge	642	22.65	Use all
Medium rye flour	435	15.35	3⅜ cups
Warm (105°F/41°C) water	100	3.55	¼ cup + 2 Tbs.
Flour for dusting	As needed		
Maple or cabbage leaves for lining pan	As needed		

2. Combine the sponge, flour, and warm water in the mixer and use the dough hook at low (KA2) speed to mix until the dough comes together into a stiff, smooth mass that leaves the sides of the bowl, 6–8 minutes. Cover and ferment at room temperature until 1½ times its original volume, 3–4 hours.

3. Turn the dough, which will be very stiff and only slightly sticky, onto a lightly floured work surface and shape it into an oblong loaf about 12 inches/30 cm long and 4 inches/10 cm wide. Place the loaf on a baking sheet that has been lined with fresh maple or cabbage leaves, cover, and proof at room temperature until the surface of the dough shows cracks, 60–75 minutes.

4. Preheat the oven to 390°F/200°C with the baking surface in the middle. Bake until the loaf thumps when tapped with a finger and the internal temperature is at least 198°F/92°C, 50–60 minutes. Transfer to a rack, brush the crust with boiling water, cover with a towel, and cool thoroughly before slicing.

BAKER'S PERCENTAGES

INGREDIENT	G	%
Medium rye flour	655	100.00%
Water	365	55.73%
Salt	7	1.07%
Potato	135	20.61%
Rye sour culture	15	2.29%
TOTAL FORMULA	1,177	179.70%
Total flour prefermented	220	33.59%

Scalded Rye Bread

Rzhannoye Chleb s Zavarku

RUSSIA This classic Russian rye employs a scald to bring a sweetness out of the rye that's musky, tinged with bitter coffee notes. It has a crisp crust and an open, tender crumb made rustic by the weight and chewiness of the coarsely milled rye meal. Traditionally this bread was baked in a round or oval pot; I use an 8-inch/20 cm French charlotte mold, but an 8-by-3-inch/20-by-8 cm round cake pan will work just as well. As one of my testers commented, "This is a very nice balance of flavors that begs for some roast beef or smoked sausages, stone-ground mustard, sweet pickles, and hearty cheese."

RYE %:	100%
STAGES:	2-stage sponge, scald, final dough
LEAVEN:	Rye sour culture
START TO FINISH:	24–28 hours
HANDS-ON TIME:	45–50 minutes
YIELD:	One 3½ lb./1.60 kg loaf or two 1¾ lb./800 g loaves

STAGE 1 SPONGE (DAY 1, MORNING)

INGREDIENT	GRAMS	OUNCES	VOLUME	BAKER'S PERCENTAGE
Medium rye flour	135	4.75	¾ cup	100%
Warm (105°F/41°C) water	270	9.50	⅞ cup	200%
Rye sour culture (see page 35)	15	0.55	½–⅔ cup	11%

1. Mix the Stage 1 sponge ingredients by hand until incorporated, cover, and ferment at room temperature (68–72°F/20–22°C) for 10–12 hours. The sponge will be very bubbly, have a clean sour smell, and will have doubled in volume.

recipe continues

Tender and Piquant: Southern Poland

WAS surprised when I began exploring the rye breads of southern Poland, where it meets Ukraine and the northern Czech Republic. I was expecting them to resemble the dense, robust ryes of Russia. Instead I found breads that charm with their subtlety. Like other breads from rye's southern tier, these start with a blend of wheat and mostly white rye flour. The base flavor is mild yet distinctively rye-centric.

It's the additions that give the breads their character. Milk and eggs tenderize the crumb of the Milk Rye (page 309). Yogurt imparts a delicate sour to the Yogurt Rye (page 293), and buttermilk moderates the intense sour of the Polish-Ukrainian Rye (page 302). Cumin adds an astringent edge to its namesake Cumin Rye (page 290) and Zakopane Buttermilk Rye (page 299), which also features the peppery punch of nigella seeds. Sunflower seeds provide a rich, nutty-sweet coating to the Sunflower Seed Rolls (page 305).

Cumin Rye

Chleb Sandomierski

POLAND I like this rye not just for its lovely sour-savory flavor and tender crumb, but because it's one of the forerunners of the rye breads I grew up with in Brooklyn. Sandomierz lies in southern Poland just west of Ukraine, in the heart of wheat country. Before World War II, it was home to millions of Jews, many of whom came to America and brought this bread with them.

Like so many southern Polish ryes, this one uses a high percentage of white rye flour, with just enough wheat to produce a tender, airy crumb. It also features a three-stage sour build, which creates extraordinary depth of flavor that's enhanced by a subtle cumin edge. The sponge also creates enough leavening power so that the bread needs only a single rise, going directly from mixer to loaf. This bread is a more robust alternative to standard American sandwich rye, as tasty with tuna salad as it is on the outside of a Reuben sandwich.

RYE %:	**70%**
STAGES:	**3-stage sponge, final dough**
LEAVEN:	**Rye sour culture**
START TO FINISH:	**24–30 hours**
HANDS-ON TIME:	**30–40 minutes**
YIELD:	**One 1¾ lb./800 g loaf**

STAGE 1 SPONGE (DAY 1, MORNING)

INGREDIENT	GRAMS	OUNCES	VOLUME	BAKER'S PERCENTAGE
White rye flour	20	0.70	2 Tbs.	100%
Warm (105°F/41°C) water	20	0.70	4 tsp.	100%
Rye sour culture (see page 35)	10	0.35	2½ tsp.	50%

1. Mix the Stage 1 sponge ingredients by hand until incorporated, cover, and ferment at room temperature (68–72°F/20–22°C) for 5–6 hours. The sponge will be very bubbly, have a clean sour smell, and will have doubled in volume.

STAGE 2 SPONGE (DAY 1, AFTERNOON)

INGREDIENT	GRAMS	OUNCES	VOLUME	BAKER'S PERCENTAGE
Stage 1 sponge	50	1.75	Use all	100%
White rye flour	50	1.75	⅓ cup	100%
Warm (105°F/41°C) water	20	0.70	4 tsp.	40%

2. Add the Stage 2 sponge ingredients to the Stage 1 sponge and mix by hand to incorporate. Cover and ferment at room temperature until bubbly and doubled in volume, 3–4 hours.

STAGE 3 SPONGE (DAY 1, EVENING)

INGREDIENT	GRAMS	OUNCES	VOLUME	BAKER'S PERCENTAGE
White rye flour	110	3.90	¾ cup	100%
Warm (105°F/41°C) water	120	4.20	½ cup + 1 Tbs.	110%
Stage 2 sponge	120	4.20	Use all	110%

3. Add the flour and warm water to the Stage 2 sponge and mix by hand to incorporate, cover, and ferment at room temperature until doubled in volume, 2½–3 hours. Refrigerate overnight.

FINAL DOUGH (DAY 2, MORNING)

INGREDIENT	GRAMS	OUNCES	VOLUME
Stage 3 sponge	350	12.30	Use all
Warm (105°F/41°C) water	155	5.45	⅔ cup
White rye flour	165	5.80	1¼ cups
Bread flour	150	5.30	1¼ cups
Salt	8	0.30	1½ tsp.
Cumin seed, toasted and ground	5	0.20	1 Tbs.
Flour for dusting	As needed		

recipe continues

4. Combine the Stage 3 sponge, flour, buttermilk, salt, and malt powder in the bowl of a mixer and use the dough hook at low (KA2) speed to mix until smooth and even, 8–10 minutes. Cover and ferment at room temperature until visibly expanded, 20–30 minutes.

5. Turn the dough out onto a well-floured work surface, knead until smooth, making sure to keep your hands and the dough surface floured, then form into a football-shaped loaf. Place on a well-floured peel, if using a baking stone, or on a parchment-lined baking sheet. Cover and proof at room temperature until the surface of the dough shows cracking, 2–2½ hours.

6. Preheat the oven to 450°F/230°C with the baking surface in the middle and a steam pan (see page 76) on a lower shelf. Slash the loaf lengthwise and bake with steam for 7 minutes. Remove the steam pan, reduce the temperature to 385°F/200°C, and bake until the crust is a rich brown color, the bread thumps when tapped with a finger, and the internal temperature is at least 198°F/92°C, 40–45 minutes. Transfer to a rack, brush immediately with boiling water, and cool thoroughly before cutting.

BAKER'S PERCENTAGES

INGREDIENT	G	%
TOTAL FLOUR	765	100.00%
Medium rye flour	455	59.48%
Bread flour	310	40.52%
Water	410	53.59%
Buttermilk	125	16.34%
Salt	14	1.83%
Rye sour	25	3.27%
Malt powder	35	4.58%
TOTAL FORMULA	1,374	179.61%
Total flour prefermented	455	59.48%

Sunflower Seed Rolls

Bułki Pszenno-Zytnie z Słonecznikiem

POLAND These yeasted white rye and wheat rolls showcase the sweet nuttiness of the grains and the rich crunch of the sunflower seeds both within and outside their crust. The dough starts out soft and very sticky but becomes much easier to work once it's floured. Their understated flavor and smooth, tender crumb make them perfect as dinner rolls or accompaniments to almost everything from roasts to cured meats and fish, from strong cheeses to honey and homemade preserves.

RYE %:	**57%**
STAGES:	**Straight dough**
LEAVEN:	**Yeast**
START TO FINISH:	**2½-3 hours**
HANDS-ON TIME:	**30–40 minutes**
YIELD:	**Sixteen 2½ oz./70 g rolls**

DOUGH

INGREDIENT	GRAMS	OUNCES	VOLUME	BAKER'S PERCENTAGE
White rye flour	400	14.10	2⅞ cups	57.14%
Bread flour	300	10.60	2⅛ cups	42.86%
Warm (105°F/41°C) water	450	15.85	2 cups	64.29%
Instant yeast	7	0.25	1¾ tsp.	1.00%
Honey	21	0.75	1 Tbs.	3.00%
Salt	6	0.20	1 tsp.	0.86%
Sunflower seeds	80	2.80	½ cup	11.43%
TOTAL FORMULA	1,264	44.55		180.57%
Total flour	700	24.70		100.00%
Flour for dusting	As needed			
Sunflower seeds for coating	80	2.80	½ cup	

recipe continues

1. Combine the flours in the mixer, make a well in the center, and pour in about half of the water, along with the yeast and honey. Stir gently to combine, bringing in enough flour from the sides to form a slurry the consistency of pancake batter. Cover and ferment at room temperature (68–72°F/20–22°C) until expanded and bubbly, 15–20 minutes.

2. Add the remaining water and the salt to the sponge and use the paddle at low (KA2) speed until the dough is partially developed, 2–3 minutes. Switch to the dough hook, add the sunflower seeds, and continue mixing at low (KA2) speed until the dough is fully developed and leaves the sides of the bowl, 6–8 minutes. Cover and ferment at room temperature until the dough has visibly expanded, 15–20 minutes.

3. Spread the sunflower seeds for coating on a plate or small baking sheet. Turn the dough, which will be soft, elastic, and somewhat sticky, onto a well-floured work surface and knead back to its original volume. Divide it into sixteen pieces, each weighing about 75 g/2¾ oz. Shape each into a ball, flatten slightly, and coat both sides with sunflower seeds. Place 1–2 inches/2.5–5 cm apart on parchment-lined baking sheet, cover, and proof at room temperature until doubled in volume, 60–75 minutes.

4. Preheat the oven to 350°F/180°C and bake the rolls until the tops turn a golden brown, 35–40 minutes. Transfer to a rack and cool thoroughly.

Sunflower Seed Rolls showcase the sweet nuttiness of the seeds that fill the tender white rye–wheat crumb and surround the crust. Sour cherry preserves complement the sweetness of this yeasted bite.

TOPPING

INGREDIENT	GRAMS	OUNCES	VOLUME
Caraway seed	7	0.25	1 Tbs.
Kosher salt	14	0.50	1 Tbs.

7. Preheat the oven to 445°F/230°C with a steam pan (see page 76) and the baking surface in the middle. Use a sharp knife or razor blade to slash each roll twice diagonally to a depth of ¼–½ inch/0.6–1.25 cm, spray or brush with water, and sprinkle first with caraway seeds and then with kosher salt. Bake until medium brown, about 20 minutes, then transfer to a rack to cool.

BAKER'S PERCENTAGES

INGREDIENT	G	%
TOTAL FLOUR	503	100.00%
AP Flour	240	47.72%
Medium rye flour	150	29.82%
Cracked wheat	83	16.50%
White rye flour	30	5.96%
Water	413	82.11%
Salt	14	2.78%
Instant yeast	4	0.80%
Pumpkinseeds	30	5.96%
Sunflower seeds	30	5.96%
Flaxseed	30	5.96%
Syrup	5	0.99%
Rye sour culture	9	1.79%
TOTAL FORMULA	1,038	206.34%
Rye flour prefermented	90	17.91%
AP flour prefermented	75	14.93%
Total flour prefermented	165	32.84%

Weinheim Carrot Rye

Weinheimer Möhrenbrot

GERMANY This bread from the southwest German state of Baden-Württemburg is a study in contrasts. Carrots and scalded oats add sweetness to a mild wheat-rye crumb that segues into an understated sour finish. The sunflower, pumpkin, and flax seeds contribute richness and delicate crunch. Green, brown, and pale gray seeds and bright orange shreds of grated carrot stand out against a background of pale orange. Its contrasts make it an ideal pairing with almost any food, from sweet to savory; frankly, I like it all by itself.

RYE %:	**39%**
STAGES:	**Sponge, scald, final dough**
LEAVEN:	**Rye sour culture, yeast**
START TO FINISH:	**18–21 hours**
HANDS-ON TIME:	**30–45 minutes**
YIELD:	**One 2.2 lb./1 kg loaf**

SPONGE (DAY 1, EVENING)

INGREDIENT	GRAMS	OUNCES	VOLUME	BAKER'S PERCENTAGE
White rye flour	130	4.60	1 cup	100%
Warm (105°F/41°C) water	120	4.25	½ cup	92%
Rye sour culture (see page 35)	13	0.45	1 Tbs.	10%

1. Mix the sponge ingredients by hand until incorporated, cover, and ferment at room temperature (68–72°F/20–22°C) overnight, 15–18 hours. The sponge will be very bubbly, have a clean sour smell, and will have tripled in volume.

recipe continues

Finely grated carrots and a medley of pumpkin, sunflower, and flax seeds create **Weinheim Carrot Rye**, a bread that's not just visually striking but also rich in contrasting flavors and textures.

SCALD (DAY 1, EVENING)

INGREDIENT	GRAMS	OUNCES	VOLUME	BAKER'S PERCENTAGE
Sunflower seeds	34	1.20	¼ cup	100%
Boiling water	160	5.65	⅔ cup	471%
Pumpkinseeds	30	1.05	¼ cup	88%
Flaxseed	30	1.05	3 Tbs.	88%
Rolled oats	25	0.90	⅓ cup	74%
Stale rye bread, crumbled	25	0.90	¼ cup	74%

2. In a separate bowl, combine the scald ingredients, cover, and let cool to room temperature, 2–3 hours, then refrigerate 13–16 hours.

FINAL DOUGH (DAY 2, MORNING)

INGREDIENT	GRAMS	OUNCES	VOLUME
Scald	304	10.75	Use all
Bread flour	250	8.80	1¾ cups
Medium rye flour	45	1.60	⅓ cup
Warm (105°F/41°C) water	80	2.85	⅓ cup
Salt	11	0.40	2 tsp.
Instant yeast	2	0.10	¾ tsp.
Sponge	263	9.25	Use all
Carrots, coarsely grated	100	3.55	¾ cup
Rolled oats for dusting/coating	As needed		

3. Add the scald, flours, water, salt, and yeast to the sponge. Use the dough hook at low (KA2) speed to mix until well blended, 6–8 minutes, scraping down the bowl as needed. Add the carrots and mix until distributed evenly, 2–3 minutes. Cover and ferment at room temperature until the dough has visibly expanded, 45–60 minutes.

recipe continues

Westphalian Pumpernickel

Westfälischer Pumpernickel

GERMANY Legend has it that pumpernickel came into being during the Middle Ages, when the wife of a Westphalian baker named Nikolaus Müller forgot to take the rye bread out of the oven. When her husband finally removed the loaves hours later, both were amazed to discover that the bread was not only edible but also dense, sweet and extraordinary.

Recipes for "Westphalian pumpernickel" abound. Most of them include sweeteners, seeds, leavenings, and a variety of other ingredients, none of which belong: by German law, pumpernickel must consist of rye, water, and salt—nothing more.

The secret to this bread's exceptional flavor and deep black color is a long scald followed by a low-temperature bake—steaming, really—that can last anywhere from 16 to 36 hours. During both scald and bake, the rye meal swells and gelatinizes and enzyme activity produces an intense, musky sweetness that takes on a slightly burnt edge as the sugars caramelize during baking.

Sliced thin, this bread has the power to enhance everything it touches—from dilled cucumber to a ripe chèvre, from the delicate salt of salmon caviar to well-aged prosciutto—without giving up any of its own unique character.

RYE %:	**100%**
STAGES:	**Scald, final dough**
LEAVEN:	**None**
START TO FINISH:	**36–40 hours**
HANDS-ON TIME:	**30–45 minutes**
YIELD:	**One 4 lb./1.80 kg loaf**

SCALD (DAY 1, AFTERNOON)

INGREDIENT	GRAMS	OUNCES	VOLUME	BAKER'S PERCENTAGE
Coarse rye meal	750	26.50	4¾ cups	100%
Boiling water	750	26.50	3⅙ cups	100%

1. Rinse the mixer with boiling water to warm it, then combine the scald ingredients, cover, and let stand at room temperature (68–72°F/20–22°C) for 16–18 hours.

FINAL DOUGH (DAY 2, MORNING)

INGREDIENT	GRAMS	OUNCES	VOLUME
Coarse rye meal	350	12.35	2¼ cups
Salt	12	0.42	2 tsp.
Scald	1,500	53.00	Use all
Vegetable shortening for pan	As needed		

2. Add the rye meal and salt to the scald and use the paddle at lowest (KA1) speed to mix until the rye meal grains are broken and the dough forms an evenly hydrated, glutinous mass, 20 minutes. The dough will be extremely heavy and dense and may jump out of the mixer, so mix in batches if necessary.

3. Grease a 9-by-4-by-4-inch/23-by-10-by-10 cm Pullman loaf pan or 9-by-5-by-3-inch/27-by-13-by-8 cm loaf pan and line it with parchment (see page 74). Grease the parchment generously with vegetable shortening, then use a plastic dough scraper and wet hands to pack the dough tightly into the pan and smooth the top, making sure there are no air pockets.

4. Cover the top of the pan with lightly greased parchment and a layer of aluminum foil, crimping the foil tightly around the lip of the pan to prevent any steam from escaping during baking.

5. Put the loaf in a cold oven and set the temperature to 300°F/150°C. After 40 minutes, lower the oven temperature to 220°F/105°C and bake for an additional 24 hours—that's right, 24 hours—so that the amylase enzymes continue to sweeten the bread and the Maillard reaction (see page 65) turns it almost black.

6. When the baking is done, remove the bread from the pan, carefully remove the parchment, let cool thoroughly, and wrap the loaf in plastic. Let stand for at least 48 hours before slicing—the thinner the better.

recipe continues

BAKER'S PERCENTAGES

INGREDIENT	G	%
Coarse rye meal	1,100	100.00%
Water	750	68.18%
Salt	12	1.09%
TOTAL FORMULA	1,862	169.27%

Consisting of nothing more than coarse rye meal, water, and salt, **Westphalian Pumpernickel**'s 40-plus-hour scald and baking process liberates every iota of rye's hidden flavors and produces a dense crumb and intensely musky-sweet loaf that's unique in the world of bread. I like it with butter and salmon caviar.

Ginger-Plum Bread, shown here with butter and apricot preserves. The zing of fresh ginger is a natural foil to the intense sweet-sour of dried plums in this instant classic from German baker Peter Kapp.

Ginger-Plum Bread

Zwetschgen-Ingwer Brot

GERMANY Sweet prunes and spicy fresh ginger are a match made in heaven. So when I came across this recipe from Peter Kapp, one of Germany's most innovative bakers, I knew I had to try it. I like intense, concentrated flavors, so I dialed up the amounts of both prunes and ginger. The cracked spelt that Kapp's recipe calls for is virtually impossible to find either at retail stores or online, so I substituted cracked wheat. The result was impressive—a sweet-sour-spicy loaf with a firm, even crumb that contrasts with the crunch of the sliced almonds that top the loaf. This is a great bread to enjoy lightly toasted and topped with a thin film of sweet butter and a touch of tart preserves; anything more would just be a distraction.

RYE %:	**60%**
STAGES:	**Sponge, soaker, final dough**
LEAVEN:	**Rye sour culture, yeast**
START TO FINISH:	**16–18 hours**
HANDS-ON TIME:	**30–40 minutes**
YIELD:	**Two 2 lb./900 g loaves**

SPONGE (DAY 1, EVENING)

INGREDIENT	GRAMS	OUNCES	VOLUME	BAKER'S PERCENTAGE
Medium rye flour	300	10.60	2⅜ cups	100%
Warm (105°F/41°C) water	240	8.45	1 cup + 1 Tbs.	80%
Rye sour culture (page 35)	6	0.20	1½ tsp.	2%

1. Mix the sponge ingredients by hand until incorporated, cover, and ferment at room temperature (68–72°F/20–22°C) overnight, 12–15 hours. The sponge will be very bubbly, have a clean sour smell, and will have doubled in volume.

recipe continues

Paderborn Rye is one of Germany's best-loved breads, with an appealing flavor profile that combines the sweetness of rye, the aromatic notes of caraway, anise, fennel, and coriander, and a pleasing mild sour finish that complements the salty sweetness of smoked ham.

Paderborn Rye

Paderborner Landbrot

GERMANY My baking friend Karin, who grew up in northern Germany and now
lives in Maine, told me about this bread. It originated in the Paderborn district of
Westphalia and is a sterling example of the region's mixed wheat-rye breads. It's also
a favorite all across Germany and one that disappears quickly from bakery shelves.
Bread spice (*brotgewürz*) adds a subtle perfume to the open, delicately sour crumb.
Its glossy brown crust is dappled with row on row of dimples from a chopstick or
docking wheel. Like other Westphalian breads, Paderborner pairs beautifully with
robust stews, roasted and grilled meat and poultry, strong-flavored cheeses, and
charcuterie, like Westphalian ham.

RYE %:	**75%**
STAGES:	**Sponge, final dough**
LEAVEN:	**Rye sour culture, yeast**
START TO FINISH:	**15–18 hours**
HANDS-ON TIME:	**30–40 minutes**
YIELD:	**One 2 lb./900 g loaf**

SPONGE (DAY 1, EVENING)

INGREDIENT	GRAMS	OUNCES	VOLUME	BAKER'S PERCENTAGE
Medium rye flour	183	6.40	1⅜ cups	100%
Warm (105°F/41°C) water	183	6.40	¾ cup + 2 tsp.	100%
Rye sour culture (see page 35)	20	0.70	5 tsp.	11%

1. Mix the sponge ingredients by hand until incorporated, cover, and ferment at room
   temperature (68–72°F/20–22°C) overnight, 14–16 hours. The sponge will be very bubbly,
   have a clean sour smell, and will have doubled in volume.

recipe continues

FINAL DOUGH (DAY 2, MORNING)

INGREDIENT	GRAMS	OUNCES	VOLUME
Sponge	386	11.40	Use all
White rye flour	143	5.05	1 cup
Medium rye flour	102	3.60	¾ cup + 1 Tbs.
First clear or high-gluten flour	140	4.95	1 cup
Warm (105°F/41°C) water	249	8.80	1 cup + 5 tsp.
Salt	11	0.40	2 tsp
Instant yeast	2	0.15	⅓ tsp.
Bread spice (see page 43)	6	0.20	1 Tbs.
Flour for dusting	As needed		
Vegetable shortening for pan	As needed		

2. Combine the sponge, flours, warm water, salt, yeast, and bread spice in the mixer and use the paddle at low (KA2) speed to mix to a shaggy mass, 2–3 minutes. Then switch to the dough hook and continue mixing until the dough becomes cohesive and gathers on the hook, 6–8 minutes. Cover and ferment at room temperature until the dough has doubled in volume, 45–50 minutes.

3. Turn the dough onto a well-floured work surface and use floured hands to knead gently back to its original volume. Shape it into a log, then place it in a well-greased 9-by-4-by-4-inch/23-by-10-by-10 cm Pullman loaf pan or 9-by-5-by-3-inch/23-by-13-by-8 cm loaf pan. Cover and proof at room temperature until the top of the dough rises slightly above the rim of the pan, 80–90 minutes.

4. Preheat the oven to 480°F/250°C with a steam pan (see page 76) and the baking surface in the middle. Brush the top of the loaf with water and use a chopstick, skewer, or docking wheel to dock the top crust to a depth of ¼–½ inch/0.6–1.25 cm. Bake with steam for 20 minutes, then remove the steam pan, reduce the oven temperature to 360°F/180°C, and bake until the loaf thumps when tapped with a finger and the internal temperature is at least 198°F/92°C, 45–50 minutes. Remove from the pan, transfer to a rack, and cool thoroughly before slicing.

BAKER'S PERCENTAGES

INGREDIENT	G	%
TOTAL FLOUR	568	100.00%
Medium rye flour	285	50.18%
White rye flour	143	25.18%
First clear flour	140	24.65%
Water	432	76.06%
Salt	11	1.94%
Instant yeast	2	0.35%
Bread spice	6	1.06%
Rye sour culture	20	3.52%
TOTAL FORMULA	1,039	182.94%
Total flour prefermented	183	32.22%

FINAL DOUGH (DAY 2, MORNING)

INGREDIENT	GRAMS	OUNCES	VOLUME
Sponge	303	10.70	Use all
Scald	275	9.75	Use all
Soaker	406	14.30	Use all
Medium rye flour	200	7.05	1½ cups
Warm (105°F/41°C) water	80	2.82	⅓ cup
Instant yeast	2	0.07	⅓ tsp.
Malt syrup, light molasses, or sugar beet syrup	25	0.88	4 tsp.
Flour for dusting	As needed		
Vegetable shortening for the pan	As needed		
Rolled oats for topping	As needed		

4. Combine the sponge, scald, soaker, flour, warm water, yeast, and syrup in the mixer and use the paddle at low (KA2) speed to mix until smooth and well blended, about 6–8 minutes. Cover and ferment at room temperature until the dough has visibly expanded, 45–60 minutes.

5. Turn the dough onto a well-floured work surface and use floured hands to shape it into an oblong, then place it in a well-greased 9-by-4-by-4-inch/23-by-10-by-10 cm Pullman loaf pan or 9-by-5-by-3-inch/23-by-13-by-8 cm loaf pan. Brush the top with water, sprinkle with rolled oats, cover, and proof at room temperature until the dough reaches the rim of the pan and shows cracks or broken bubbles, 1–1½ hours.

6. Preheat the oven to 465°F/240°C with a steam pan (see page 76) and the baking surface in the middle. Bake with steam for 15 minutes, then remove the steam pan and lower the oven temperature to 390°F/200°C. Bake until the loaf thumps when tapped with a finger and the internal temperature is at least 198°F/92°C, 50–60 minutes. Remove from the pan, transfer to a rack, and let cool thoroughly before slicing.

BAKER'S PERCENTAGES

INGREDIENT	G	%
TOTAL FLOUR	500	100.00%
Coarse rye meal	300	60.00%
Medium rye flour	200	40.00%
Water	320	64.00%
Salt	14	2.80%
Instant yeast	2	0.40%
Soaker water	200	40.00%
Sunflower seeds	100	20.00%
Flaxseed	50	10.00%
Stale bread	50	10.00%
Syrup	25	5.00%
Rye sour culture	30	6.00%
TOTAL FORMULA	1,291	258.20%
Total flour prefermented	150	30.00%

Kapp, Peter, *Mein Brot: Rezepte ohne Kompromisse* (My Bread: Recipes Without Compromise), Königswinter: HEEL, 2014.

Kellner, Gerhard, *Rustikale Brote aus deutschen Landen* (Rustic Breads from German Regions), Munich: Bassermann, 2012.

Lafer, Johann, ed., *Deutschlands bester Bäcker: Rezepte & Backgeheimnisse* (Germany's Best Bakers: Recipes & Baking Secrets), Munich: Gräfe & Unzer, 2014.

Leader, Daniel, *Local Breads*, New York: W. W. Norton & Company, 2007.

Luther, Harald, ed., *Brotrezepte aus ländlichen Backstuben* (Bread Recipes from Regional Bakeries), Schwarzenbek: Cadmos Verlag, 2009.

Marder, Pawel, *Chleb domowy wypiek* (Bake Bread at Home), Warsaw: Wydawnictwo SBM Sp., 2012.

McGee, Harold, *On Food and Cooking: The Science and Lore of the Kitchen*, rev. ed., New York: Scribner, 2004.

Reinhart, Peter, *Peter Reinhart's Whole Grain Breads*, Berkeley: Ten Speed Press, 2007.

Schröder, Christine, *BROT: So backen unsere besten Bäcker* (Bread: As Baked by Our Best Bakers), Neustadt: Umschau, 2010.

Stopa, Magdalena, and Federico Caponi, *Chleb po Warszawsku* (Bread in Warsaw), Warsaw: VEDA, 2012.

Weinold-Leipold, Helene, *Brot & Brötchen* (Bread & Rolls), Munich: Bassermann, 2010.

Ingredients

Finding the various rye and specialty wheat flours is a particular challenge for home rye bakers. Some supermarket chains and large club retailers selectively carry rye flour, but it's generally only a single variety—medium or whole grain—and their wheat flours typically are limited to AP flour and bread flour. Online retailers offer a much wider variety:

The New York Bakers (www.nybakers .com), which I founded in 2009, has the broadest offering of milled rye, including white, medium, and dark rye flour; coarse, medium, and fine rye meals; malted rye; unbleached first clear flour; and several grades of high-gluten and bread flours. NYB also sells imported French linen-lined *bannetons* and imported German rattan bread forms (*brotformen*).

King Arthur Flour (www.kingarthurflour .com) sells medium and white rye flour, plus pumpernickel flour (fine rye meal) and first clear flour. They also sell Perfect Rye Flour Blend, which consists of undisclosed percentages of white and medium rye flour, pumpernickel flour, and their unbleached bread flour.

Central Milling (centralmilling.com) offers a wide range of high quality organic flours, including medium rye, 100% whole dark rye, and pumpernickel flour (fine rye meal), as well as Type 110 flour, which is equivalent to first clear flour.

Hodgson Mill whole-grain and organic whole-grain rye flours are available at selected hypermarket and club stores and online at www.hodgsonmillstore.com.

Bob's Red Mill products are widely available at specialty and some mainstream groceries. Their website (www.bobsredmill.com) sells white rye flour and organic whole-grain rye flour, as well as whole organic rye berries and medium rye meal, which they sell as pumpernickel meal.

Syrups. For cane syrup, aka light molasses, **Steen's** (www.steensyrup.com) is the standard. German sugar beet syrup (*Rübenkraut*) is available through **GermanDeli.com** (www.germandeli.com).

Utensils and Supplies

Some utensils and supplies are hard to find locally. **Food Service Warehouse** (www.foodservicewarehouse.com) and **The Webstaurant Store** (www.webstaurantstore.com) offer the gamut of professional food service equipment and supplies. For more specialized items, such as bread forms (*brotformen*) and linen-lined *bannetons*, go to **The New York Bakers** (www.nybakers.com), **brotform.com** (www.brotform.com), and **TMB Baking** (www.tmbbaking.com).

About the Author

Stanley Ginsberg is coauthor of the 2012 IACP Jane Grigson Award–winning *Inside the Jewish Bakery: Recipes and Memories from the Golden Age of Jewish Baking* (Camino Books, 2011). He grew up in post–World War II Brooklyn, where he learned to bake from his grandmothers. He pursued bread baking as a hobby as a graduate student at the University of Wisconsin, where he earned a Ph.D. in Chinese Language and Literature. After decades devoted to family and career, he returned to bread baking as his children reached adulthood and his professional responsibilities wound down.

It was during his research into the rye breads of his immigrant forebears that Stanley became aware of rye's prominent place in the social history and culinary traditions of northern, central, and eastern Europe. Over time, his exploration of traditional rye breads transformed him from a wheat-centric hobbyist craft baker into a hard-core lover of all breads rye. It also set him on the path toward writing *The Rye Baker*.

In addition to writing and baking, Stanley owns and operates The New York Bakers (nybakers.com), an e-tailer of professional and specialty ingredients, supplies, and equipment, including a wide range of rye flours. He and his wife, Sylvia Spieler Ginsberg, live in San Diego, California, and have three adult children, three beautiful granddaughters, and one lovable standard poodle.